THE OLD
CHINA HANDS

CHARLES G. FINNEY

DRAWINGS BY

Arthur Shilstone

THE OLD

CHINA HANDS

Doubleday & Company, Inc.

Garden City, New York,

1961

The stories *The Night Crawler*, *Anabasis in Minor Key*, and *Private Prince*, appeared originally in *The New Yorker*. *Anabasis* appears here as *The Foot Cavalry*.

915.1
F

First Edition

Dedicated to

MARIE

Officers Serving in China with the 15th Infantry,
Official Roster, Mar. 1927

Rank (then)	Name	Assignment	Highest rank ever	Remarks
Col.	Newell, Isaac	C.O.	Col.	Ret'd 1930
Lt. Col.	Marshall, George C.	Ex. Off.	Gen. of the Army	C of S, Sec. St. & Def. Deceased
Majs.	Stilwell, Joseph W.	2nd Batt.	Gen.	Deceased
	Harding, Edwin F.	Unassgd.	Maj. Gen.	
	Doe, Jens A.	3rd Batt.	Maj. Gen.	
Capts.	Patrick, Edwin	P&T Off.	Maj. Gen.	Killed WW II
	Poage, Robert O.	Pers. Adj.	?	Died prior WW II
	Anderson, G. A.	Adj.	Col.	
	Tuttle, William B.	Serv. Co.	Col.	Deceased
	Hayne, Frank B.	G Co.	Col.	
	Pearson, Frank J.	K Co.	Col.	
	Coughlin, Jos. V.	F Co.	Col.	Deceased
	Forney, Leslie R.	H Co.	Col.	
	Schwab, John S.	Unassgd.	Capt.	Died prior WW II
	Champeny, A. S.	L Co.	Brig. Gen.	
	Crowell, Harold B.	Sup. Off.	Col.	
	Harvey, Leigh I.	E Co.	Maj.	Ret'd in '31
	Evans, Will H.	Unassgd.	Capt.	Ret'd in '29
	Willingham, C. M.	I Co.	Col.	
	Williamson, R. J.	M Co.	Col.	Deceased
	Buracker, S. L.	Unassgd.	Col.	
1st Lts.	Barber, Henry A.	Unassgd.	Brig. Gen.	Deceased

Rank (then)	Name	Assignment	Highest rank ever	Remarks
	Robertson, S. C.	G Co.	Maj.	Ret'd prior WW II
	Burrowes, Robert M.	E Co.	1st Lt.	Died China '28
	De Pass, Morris B.	Adj; 2nd Bn.	Col.	
	McCammon, John E.	Serv. Co.	Col.	
	Christian, T. H.	F Co.	Maj.	Died prior WW II
	Pomerene, Joel D.	Hq. Co.	Col.	Deceased
	Cookson, Forrest B.	M Co.	Col.	
	Adams, Dwight L.	M Co.	1st Lt.	Died in '35
	Snodgrass, E. H.	Serv. Co.	Col.	
	Howard, Thomas R.	F Co.	Col.	
	Harris, Fred. M.	K Co.	Brig. Gen.	
	McQuarrie, C. M.	I Co.	Brig. Gen.	
2nd Lts.	Maloney, George H.	K Co.	Lt. Col.	
	Pierce, James R.	Adj; 3rd Bn.	Maj. Gen.	Died prior WW II
	Hilliard, L. L.	H Co.	Lt. Col.	
	Gunn, Damon M.	I Co.	Col.	Ret'd early WW II
	Ridings, Eugene W.	G Co.	Maj. Gen.	
	Timberman, T. S.	L Co.	Maj. Gen.	
	Storck, Louis J.	H Co.	Col.	Killed in WW II
	Boone, Joseph W.	L Co.	Col.	
Capt. (Chap.)	Miller, Luther D.	Chaplain	Maj. Gen.	Chief of Chaplains

Maj.	Ridgway, Matthew B.	Gen.	C of S, Army
Capt.	Williams, L. L.	Lt. Gen.	
Maj.	McCunniff, Dennis E.	Brig. Gen.	Deceased
Capt.	Brann, Donald W.	Maj. Gen.	Deceased
1st Lt.	Butler, Frederick B.	Brig. Gen.	
1st Lt.	Gallagher, Philip E.	Maj. Gen.	
1st Lt.	Honnen, George	Maj. Gen.	
Capt.	Cushman, Horace O.	Brig. Gen.	
Capt.	Steele, Paul	Col.	

AFTER DATE OF ROSTER

Rank *(then)*	Name	Highest rank *ever*	Remarks
1st Lt.	Jenkins, Reuben E.	Lt. Gen.	
2nd Lt.	Boatner, Hayden L.	Maj. Gen.	
Capt.	Deane, John R.	Maj. Gen.	Headed Military Mission to Moscow, WW II
Capt.	Whitcomb, John C.	Col.	
Lt. Col.	Cummins, Joseph M.	Maj. Gen.	Deceased

Acknowledgments

After General William Tecumseh Sherman had published his memoirs, a number of his friends were happy to point out what they assured him were glaring inconsistencies between what he had written and what the historic facts were. Sherman thought it over for a while, and then said something like this: "Well, dammit, they're *my* memoirs, and I'm going to let them stand as written." And I feel the same way, for once something has been fixed in one's mind more or less for thirty years it has taken on for that person the concreteness of truth, and the citation of a lousy, contradictory *fact* isn't enough to persuade one to revise his memory of it.

In addition to my own concept about the doings of the warlords in North China circa 1924–30, I have relied on the Encyclopedia Britannica for help in untangling their machinations. (A complete untangling shall be forever beyond my ability.) Then, too, I gleaned much information from the 15th Infantry's *Year Book* of 1924–25, edited by (then) Lieutenant L. L. Williams. (He is now a lieutenant general, retired.) This yearbook was made available to me by Major General (retired) Philip E. Gallagher, who was at the time of the yearbook's compiling a first lieutenant. As a captain, Gallagher made the speech when the 15th Infantry presented its memorial gate to the Infantry School at Fort Benning in 1939. The *general* has given me permission to quote the *captain's* words in the story herein titled *The Gate*, and I salute him for so doing. As to the inscription on the gate, the gate's location in Benning, a copy of Captain Gallagher's speech, etc., I am indebted to Major Rolfe L. Hillman, Jr., who at this writing is stationed at the post.

Another valuable source of inspiration has been Major (now major general) Edwin F. Harding's book of poems, *Lays of the*

Mei Kuo Y'ing Pan. Harding, at the time he wrote it, was the poet laureate of the 15th Infantry. His *Tutullius at the Bridge* recounts another exploit of Captain Wild Bill Tuttle during the stirring days of '24.

Then there is that strange little booklet, *Customs of the Fifteenth U. S. Infantry.* It was brought out the year after I left China (1930) under the aegis of the then regimental commander, Colonel James D. Taylor. The copy I have is the facsimile reproduction published by Hope Farm Press of Cornwallville, New York. I mention *Customs* in the story *The Orderly.*

For the description of the Civil War musket which Digby Hand fired in *The Ratel Hunt,* I am indebted to *The Gun Digest,* edited by John T. Amber. To the same publication I am indebted for material about Townsend Whelen and his days with the 15th. Indeed, it was from Colonel Whelen's article in *The Gun Digest,* "Days of the Krag," that the material was taken. Colonel Whelen is one of the grand old men of the U. S. Army. Nearing ninety, he still shoots every week.

Finally, I am indebted to Major General (retired) H. B. Lewis and Colonel (retired) John C. Whitcomb, who, as young officers, were on the hike which is described herein under the title *The Foot Cavalry.* Both were kind enough to write me after the story appeared in *The New Yorker* magazine where it was titled *Anabasis in Minor Key,* and, in subsequent correspondence, elaborated on the doings of that memorable day. H. B. Lewis, then a major, was on General Castner's staff, and John C. Whitcomb, then a captain, had just arrived in China. They both completed the hike, and neither of them has ever forgotten the last fifteen miles.

The names of the enlisted men used in this book are fictitious, and the enlisted men themselves are syntheses of several men rather than portraits of individuals. As to the officers, the names of Marshall, Stilwell, Castner, Newell, Butler, Tuttle, Burrowes, Dabney are all in history—any attempt at disguise would be silly.

General Lewis has furnished me with a list of officers who served with the 15th while I was there. These were *regimental,* not *staff,* officers. Assuming that the old China days were, in a way, formative in their careers, they didn't do so badly. I think it's rather impressive, considering that the 15th in those days was only a skeleton outfit. These are the ranks the field officers and the company officers of 1927–30 held at the time of their deaths or as of 1960.

General of the Army (5 stars)
George C. Marshall

General (4 stars)
Joseph W. Stilwell
Matthew B. Ridgway

Lieutenant General (3 stars)
L. L. Williams
Reuben E. Jenkins

Major General (2 stars)
Edwin F. Harding
Jens A. Doe
Edwin Patrick
James R. Pierce
Eugene W. Ridings
T. S. Timberman
Luther D. Miller (chief of chaplains)
Donald W. Brann
Philip E. Gallagher
George Honnen
Hayden L. Boatner
John R. Deane
Joseph M. Cummins

Brigadier General (1 star)
A. S. Champeny
Henry A. Barber
Frederick M. Harris
C. M. McQuarrie
Dennis E. McCunniff
Frederick B. Butler
Horace O. Cushman

Comparisons are hardly in order, but I wonder what other infantry regiment of those days can boast of such an alumni list?

Prefatory Note

They won their first campaign streamer at Shiloh in 1862, their latest in Korea in 1953. In between, they gathered more battle flags at:

Mississippi
Alabama
Tennessee
Kentucky
Murfreesboro
Chickamauga
Chattanooga
Atlanta——where they fought against the Southerners;

New Mexico——where they fought against the Utes;

Luzon——where they fought against the Insurrectos;

Algeria
Tunisia
Sicily
Italy
Southern France
Rhineland
Ardennes-Alsace
Central Europe——where they fought against the Nazis;

CCF Intervention (Chinese Communist Forces)
First UN Counteroffensive
CCF Spring Offensive
UN Summer–Fall Offensive
Second Korean Winter
Korean Summer–Fall 1952
Third Korean Winter
Korean Summer–Fall 1953——where they fought against the Red
   Koreans and the Red Chinese.

At this writing (1960), ninety-eight years after Shiloh, they are part of the First Battle Group in Germany. Over the years they have collected twenty Congressional Medals of Honor, barrels of Purple Hearts, carloads of other decorations. They began their fighting history with muzzle-loading muskets; now they have nuclear bombs.

They are, of course, the members of the 15th U. S. Infantry Regiment. But where were they during the First World War? Why no battle streamers from that grand dispute? Well, they were in China, sitting it out, as it were. They were stationed in Tientsin from 1912 to 1938, guarding American lives and property. That's where they got their name "Old China Hands" and their regimental insigne, a blue and white shield with the Imperial Dragon rampant and the motto "Can Do."

It seems perhaps surprising that so little has been written about their twenty-six-year stay in North China. But then hardly anything of a blood-and-thunder nature happened. They guarded bridges now and then; they set up road blocks once in a while to keep the troops of some war lord from entering the Foreign Concessions of Tientsin; they manned international trains occasionally in an attempt to keep the Peking-Mukden Railway open from Peking to the sea. But that was all. They never traded bullets and lives with a foe. They were simply a nine-hundred-man symbol of American military power, living in Tientsin almost as "guests" of the Chinese.

When I decided to enlist in the Army in 1927, I didn't even know that the U.S.A. had a regiment stationed in China. I had thought to sign up for Hawaii or Panama or the Philippines, but the recruiting corporal said: "Why don't you go to China, fella? They're taking guys now with high school diplomas. All you do is goldbrick there—no fatigue duty or anything. Tailor-made uniforms. Best chow in the Army. There ain't no prohibition there. A man can drink his fool head off. I wouldn't mind going myself, only the wife wouldn't stand for it."

So, because I wanted to be far, far away, as far away as possible from the railroad shops where I had been working, I enlisted for China. A nucleus of other enlistees and myself—all from the Midwest—gathered at Fort Leavenworth, Kansas, for the trip to our embarkation point in San Francisco, and not one of us knew anything about Tientsin, where it was located in China, or what life there was like. Neither did any of the garrison troops at Leavenworth. It wasn't until we reached Angel Island in San Francisco Bay that we encountered men who had been there. And their views were conflicting. "Hell hole on earth," said one. "Best place in the world to soldier," said another. "It's okay if you like liquor and women," said a third.

"How are the chances of promotion?" we asked.

"There ain't any. The sergeants all go over in grade, and they don't ever leave till they get run out, and then another sergeant from the States replaces 'em. Some of them have been there twelve years. Same way with the corporals. Soon as a guy gets his two stripes—which ain't often—he gets him a squaw and shacks up. Then *he* stays till they run *him* out. Sometimes a guy can make first-class private after three or four years, but it ain't too likely."

"Yes, but what's it like—what's the city like?"

"It stinks. Everything in China stinks."

"Yes, but how about the duty—is it hard?"

"There ain't any duty to speak of. You drill in the mornings and get the afternoons off. You catch guard every nine days. But you don't do any fatigue, and you don't do any KP; you hire coolies to do it for you. You don't make your own bed; you don't shine your own shoes; you don't fill your own canteen; you don't shave yourself; the Chink coolies do it for you. You get waited on hand and foot."

"How come you left?"

"It ain't a white man's country."

The first white man to see Tientsin was Marco Polo, and that was back around the year 1290 when the city had only twenty or thirty thousand inhabitants and was clustered around the juncture of the Grand Canal and the Hai River. Marco, who was at that time a high official in Peking with a seat near the Dragon Throne, was not too impressed. Some six hundred and thirty-odd years later, when I first saw Tientsin, it was a city of about 900,000. In 1946 its census stood at 1,707,670. Nowadays (1960) it's crowding 3,000,000.

Well, there is nothing to stop Tientsin from growing; some day, conceivably, it could become the largest city in the world—unless, of course, nuclear warfare wipes it from the face of the earth. It sits on a huge alluvial plain and straddles two rivers and the Grand Canal, so it has plenty of water. Railroads pierce it. Some of the greatest coal deposits in existence are nearby. The alluvial plain will grow anything. In Marco Polo's day it might have been a hick town on a riverbank, but it's not any more.

By 1850, Tientsin had become the chief port of North China, doing business by sampan from Taku Bar some sixty miles down the river. When a rebellion broke out in 1858 (there were always rebellions in those days) the city was occupied by British and French troops, for the British and French were already trading there; and it is the law that cannons follow merchants. In 1860 the city was formally "opened," and foreign trade permits were granted to Britain, Belgium, France, Italy, Japan, and Russia.

Buying and selling were pursued peacefully, but Tientsin was still a Chinese city enclosed in a turreted Chinese wall. Then, in 1900, the Boxer Rebellion broke out, and Tientsin was never to be the same again. The Boxers besieged Tientsin and captured it. They also besieged the foreign legations in Peking, but found themselves pretty much fought off there. An international relief force of Russian, German, Japanese, British, French, Italian, and American troops was formed: the legation siege at Peking was raised; Tientsin was recaptured. The rebellion was put down, and the Boxer Protocols were drawn up. Under these Protocols, China agreed that foreign troops could remain in Tientsin to guard foreign property.

Tientsin had taken quite a battering during the rebellion. After the fighting ended, the turreted city wall (the storming of which had been tough on the white soldiers) was pulled down, and the city was remade on modern lines. The rebuilt metropolis was no longer Chinese. It was a beautiful mixture. Britain, France, Germany, Russia, Japan, and Italy each took a portion of the city—or a Concession, as it was called—and built it up under their own ideas, but also under a master, over-all plan. China, under the terms of the Protocols, provided the money for the rebuilding. The United States was offered a Concession and reparation money. But we turned the Concession down, and diverted the money to the education of Chinese students in American universities.

The new Tientsin burgeoned. The main thoroughfare through the Concessions started out as Kaiser Wilhelmstrasse, became Victoria Road when it entered the British territory, Rue de France when it entered the French, and Via Italia when it entered the Italian. The Russian Concession was across the Hai Ho, and the Russians, being occupied elsewhere, never did much with it except to lay out a big, lovely park which promptly was allowed to lapse into a state of dismal neglect. The Japanese Concession did not touch on the main thoroughfare.

What was left of old Tientsin became known as the Native City. Down came everything made of mud, and up went new things made of brick and concrete. When it was done, it was the finest "native city" in the Orient.

Under British supervision Tientsin became the best-policed city in the Orient, also. Britons acted as chiefs, Sikhs as sergeants, and Chinese as patrolmen. Under British supervision, the Peking-Mukden Railway—Tientsin's major carrier—was already one of the best railroads in the world.

Tientsin became beautiful, not in the sense that Peking with age-old walls and halls and temples was beautiful, but in the sense that modern planning could make a brand-new city beautiful. Canals traversed it. Macadamized streets dissected it. Parks dotted it. American business blossomed, but there were no American troops in Tientsin. They had been pulled out after the Boxers had been defeated.

On October 10, 1911, a bomb explosion in Hankow, far away from Tientsin, ignited another rebellion. By Christmas, the dynasty of the Manchus, two hundred sixty-seven years old, was ground into the dust, the Dragon Throne was empty, and Dr. Sun Yat-sen was seated as president of China. And during that month of October, the 15th Infantry's First Battalion was on the seas, sailing for China; and the regiment's twenty-six-year stay in Tientsin was about to begin.

The 15th Infantry had been in Tientsin fifteen years when I joined it, and its customs were established. It was housed in brick stucco barracks in the walled American Compound in the First Special Area—the name given the German Concession after the Germans abandoned their Tientsin holdings in the First World War. Kaiser Wilhelmstrasse had become Woodrow Wilson Street. Commanding officers and company officers had come and gone; enlisted men had completed their tours of duty and had been replaced by other enlisted men; blue uniforms had been changed to olive drab; the Browning water-cooled machine gun had replaced the Vickers-Maxim; but the regimental continuity had been established, and Tientsin was the 15th Infantry's "home."

Garrisons of British, French, Japanese, and Italians also had their "homes" in Tientsin in their appropriate Concessions; and they, too, had established their customs. Tientsin was an international city guarded by international troops; the troops were there not to impose order on Tientsin, but to prevent disorder from flowing in. It was the only such city in the world. It was rich and it was booming. And so it still was when I left. Later, the Japanese conquered it, only to lose it to the Chinese Nationalists who, in turn, lost it to the Chinese Communists. Well, the Hai Ho still runs through it, and, I suppose, the flowers still bloom in Victoria Park. As I said before, it may someday become the largest city in the world. It has always kept growing, even under its startling variety of rulers. Tientsin seems to thrive on war.

When I left China late in 1929, I had the beginnings of a book with me, which later here in Tucson I remolded into *The Circus of Dr. Lao*. Then I put China more or less out of mind and my mind became occupied with other things. Now, after thirty years—why, I cannot say, except that after thirty years one is truly "retired" from the Army even if one has not spent all the thirty years in it—Tientsin and the 15th Infantry of the old China have come back to my mind in pleasant memory.

Three of the stories which follow were first published in *The New Yorker* magazine and appear here in slightly altered form. Although the old China hands were anything but Boy

Scouts, I have thought it best not to stress at all their venery. If I set my mind to it, I could do it, of course. I could shovel out filth and profanity by the truckload. But everybody nowadays knows how babies are made and has a fair knowledge—even though not necessarily a working knowledge—of the Left Bank mechanics of the act of love. So let us not clutter up our pages with dirty memories. Let us, instead, as does the fastidious sun dial, only mark the shining hours.

Tucson—Summer, Autumn 1960   CGF

Contents

Tientsin

THE NEW BOOK

1 ✺

After the ring matches were over that night, little Calhoun Shaw and I left the Recreation Hall and went to the Café Genève for a beer. The 15th Infantry's great heavyweight, Reeves, had just flattened the pride of Great Britain's First Welsh Border Regiment, and it seemed a time to celebrate. We would, of course, have gone to the Genève even if Reeves had lost, but his victory seemed to give a special impetus to our visit. In the Genève we met Robert Counts; he had come to China in 1925 (I in 1927, and little Shaw in 1928). Counts had re-enlisted for a second three-year term in Tientsin and wore on his sleeves the single stripe of a first-class private.

"Who won?" he asked.

"Reeves . . . knockout in the third."

"Naturally. Naturally. Reeves, the fair-haired boy. He always wins. But there was a guy here once in the 15th that could have handled Mr. Reeves. Course, he wasn't here long, and it's a good thing he's gone; but he could have handled Reeves."

Neither Shaw nor I said anything.

"His name was Alaska Canning," said Counts. "He wasn't so tall as Reeves, but he was bigger around, and his hands hung clear down to his knees. He came over on the same boat I was on back in '25. God, how I hated him. So did everybody else. One time off Luzon on the last stretch to China, five or six of us got tired of the way Canning was acting and we ganged up on him and laid him out. Should of done it right at the beginning, I guess. He laid out two of us first, but we finally got him down and stomped him. He stayed pretty gentle for the rest of the trip—which he made in the sick bay. Man, that was the old army in those days! High-collared blouses, canvas leggings, dinky little garrison caps.

"But I was telling you about Alaska Canning, and how he could of licked this fair-haired hero Reeves. Canning was the one who got us the name 'Scum of the Earth' when we docked at Honolulu on the way over. They wouldn't let us off the transport, and everybody was feeling mean—Canning meanest of all. The old *Thomas*—that was the ship—the U.S. got her from the Germans after the war and re-christened her the *Thomas*, and put her in transport service. She was a good boat—lots of deck space.

"Everybody was sick as all getout from the day we sailed from Frisco till the day before we reached Oahu, but then we perked up quite a bit. There were five hundred men aboard going to Hawaii and three hundred going to the Philippines and a hundred and fifty of us going to China. That made nine hundred and fifty seasick guys; man, did the old *Thomas* smell! They gave us beans, pickles, and onions for our first meal out, and those beans, pickles, and

onions was sprayed topside and bottomside before we got
done being seasick. Alaska Canning had been just as seasick
as the rest of us and, except for smacking three guys the
first day out, had been fairly peaceable. You see, Canning
was a great one for smacking guys. You'd jostle him in the
chow line and he'd take a smack at you. He didn't like
where you were standing at the rail, and he'd smack you.
But mostly between the Golden Gate and Diamond Head he
was too sick to do much smacking. However, like I said,
everybody perked up the day before we reached Oahu, and
Canning had managed to smack about six guys before we
docked.

"Well, we pulled into the pier at Honolulu, and we figured
they'd let us off the boat after inspection and let us wander
around the city some and see what it was like to walk on dry
land again. But nope, they didn't. They unloaded real quick
the guys that were bound for Hawaii, and they let the officers
and their ladies get off down a special gangplank; but the
rest of us they kept on. They said somebody was in the
sick bay, and they figured it might be contagious. We got
there at eight in the morning and would sail at eight the
next.

"We were mad as hell naturally, but they had MPs on
the wharf, guys from Schofield Barracks packing pistols, and
there wasn't anything we could do about it.

"Little naked native kids came around in canoes and dove
for pennies that we threw in for them. One of our fellows
said, 'Hell, if them kids can swim there, why cain't we?'
And he shucked off his clothes and dove in from the rail of
the *Thomas*. He was a good swimmer and he had a fine
time horsing around in the water with the native kids. Then
the MPs saw him and one of them hauled out his pistol and
fired a couple of shots mighty, mighty close to him in the
water. That ended that; he clum up a rope we let down to
him, and somebody took his name, and I guess he got

court-martialed later. He was going to the Philippines and I never got to know him very well.

"The Hawaiian natives made a kind of firewater that they called *okolehao*—maybe you guys tasted it when your boat stopped there—and some of it, a lot of it, got on board the *Thomas*. You know how it's done: Vendors come alongside—the MPs let 'em through—and they've got baskets tied to ropes, and they toss the ropes up to you, and you pull the baskets up and put money in 'em and let 'em down, and for that money you get soda pop and cake and fruit and stuff like that. Well, one of the guys—he'd done a hitch in Hawaii before—knew about this *okolehao*, and he spoke the Hawaiian lingo and he got a vendor to get him some. I know damn well some of the MPs got bribed, but anyway, after a while the *okolehao* was coming onto the *Thomas* by the barrel. Man, that is the most powerful stuff ever created! Alaska Canning, this guy I was telling you about, got a bottle of it—I think he just jerked it away from somebody else—and he took to the *oke* like a gull takes to fish. He was onery enough when he was sober; when he got fired up on the *oke* he was just plain impossible. I stayed to hell away from him.

"Well, that evening just at sundown, an army band came along to serenade us. And they had some hula girls to dance for us, and stuff like that. We were cooped up on the *Thomas*, you know, and all this entertainment was staged below us on the pier. They even brought along a chaplain, and he prayed for us and got us to sing a hymn or two. Turned out it was Sunday, but nobody had paid any attention.

"Well, like I say, I had been staying out of Alaska Canning's way; I had had a nip or two of *okolehao* myself, but I wasn't feeling belligerent. I was just standing there at peace with myself listening to the hymn singing. But along comes Canning, practically on his hands and knees he's so drunk, and he's got an empty pop bottle in each hand. He generally cussed a lot, but he wasn't cussing now. He was talking like the chaplain talked: 'I have seen mine enemy. I have seen mine ancient enemy, and the Lord hath delivered him into mine hands.'

"Then he quit talking like the chaplain and began to talk like his old self again. 'See that crinkly-haired son of a bitch playing the piccolo down there? He done me dirt in Nome, Alaska. He done me dirt in Skagway; and now it's payday for big boy Canning. I'm gonna part his crinkly hair for him for keeps.' And he steadied himself at the rail with one hand, and with the other hand let fly with one of his pop bottles, and he hit the piccolo player a bull's-eye right in the crown of his campaign hat. That stopped the hymn singing. The piccolo player fell down, and blood ran all over his face; and there was hell to pay.

"Officers came, tough MP officers, and they swarmed over the *Thomas* and put every one of us under arrest. Looking back, I reckon if I had it to do over again, I would of squealed on Canning. But I didn't and neither did the other guys who had seen him pitch his pop bottle. Later on, of course, after we got a bellyful of him for the last time and stomped his face in when the *Thomas* was off Luzon, we wondered why we hadn't, but at the time we didn't, and that was that.

"Well, they had an investigation, but couldn't prove anything except that about a third of the guys on board were hopped up on *okolehao* and any of them could of done it. But, because of the bunking arrangement and because of where we were standing on deck, they figured it was probably somebody in the China-bound group that had done it.

" 'You men,' said the major, who was bossing the hearing, 'are the scum of the earth. I'm putting a black mark by each and every one of your damnable names. And if that bands-man dies, I'm going to hang somebody.'

"Well, the bandsman didn't die, but that was the way it went the rest of the way across the Pacific. We were the scum of the earth. They wouldn't let us off at Guam when the *Thomas* stopped there. They didn't want to let us off at Manila when we reached the Philippines, but they had to because they had to clean up the ship. The medical officers ordered it. So they let us off under guard and took us up the Pasig River on barges to Fort William McKinley. And there—under guard—we stayed ten days. Crazily enough, the second day we were there, they paid each one of us ten dollars. It was after that that we piled some more scum on our names.

"Daytimes—in the mornings, that is—they'd take us out on the parade ground and put us through setting-up exer-cises and a pretense at close-order drill. In the afternoons, when it generally rained to beat hell, they tried to figure out some sort of fatigue duty for us to do. We swept floors, washed windows, lugged stuff around; anything to keep us busy. In the evenings, they slapped guards at the barracks doors and let us stew in our own juice. A lot of the fellows got into crap and poker games, and in less'n no time lost that ten dollars they'd been paid. But there was still quite a bit of money around. Hundred and fifty men times ten bucks a head is still fifteen hundred bucks.

"Well, somebody—a guard, a Filipino, I don't know who —let it be known that he'd bring in all the gin he could carry at two dollars a pint. The stuff was cheap in the Philippines. Pretty soon it was just gin all over the place. We slept on the top floor of an old wooden barracks; the mess hall and dayroom were on the ground floor. The fifth night we were there, everybody got ginned up. For a while we just horsed around and sang and hollered. But then, Canning—it was always Canning—bopped some guy and knocked him cold; and three of the guy's friends pitched into Canning. Some of the other guys thought that wasn't fair, even against Canning, so they pitched in, too, and pretty soon the whole upper deck of that old wooden barracks was a screaming hell house.

"Well, the guys on guard at the barracks doors blew their whistles, and more guards came, and officers with them; and pretty soon it seemed like the whole damn garrison of Fort William McKinley was there, trying to battle their way up the barracks stairs to get to us and beat the hell out of us.

"We barricaded the stairs. Bunks were overthrown, and tables and chairs busted, and there were black eyes and busted noses and busted knuckles all over the place. We thought they were trying to kill us, and we fought back hard.

"Every once in a while somebody would yell, 'Scum of the earth, sound off!' And we'd all sound off, and things'd get hotter and hotter. They finally brought up fire hoses, and that did it. We surrendered. Man, was that barracks a mess! They slapped a chain guard around it, guys armed with .45 Colts, standing shoulder to shoulder; and all of us still inside, of course. Then they came in with lanterns and flashlights—all the lights in the barracks were busted out by then—and they made every guy strip down and they searched for the gin. A lot of the gin was in us, of course, but they still found a lot to pour down the drain.

"It was about two o'clock in the morning, and right on the spot they made us start cleaning that barracks up. Come dawn, they skipped breakfast for us and trotted us out on the drill field for setting-up exercises instead. 'These China-bound gentlemen got to get some of the steam worked out of their systems,' said a lieutenant. Well, he worked it out of us.

"They didn't do anything more to us in the Philippines except keep that chain guard around us—and, God, how those guys on guard hated it—and no more gin got in, and the black eyes began to clear up and the busted knuckles to heal. Alaska Canning socked a couple of more guys, but nobody paid much attention to it. When the ten days were finally up—they seemed like ten years—they marched us down to the Pasig River and loaded us on barges for the trip to the *Thomas*. The lieutenant in command of the guard detail that saw us off gave us a final lecture: 'We could of locked every damn one of you up here at McKinley and throwed the key away,' he said. 'But we didn't want no more to do with you than we had to, so we're simply sending you on to your next destination. But we haven't entirely overlooked your behavior while you were our guests. We have compiled a book on every one of you, and there's a big beautiful black mark in that book against every one of your names. It will be turned over to your commanding officer in China to do with it what he sees fit.'

"Well, we piled onto the *Thomas*, and nothing much happened for a day or two until Alaska Canning bopped a guy standing ahead of him in the chow line. We didn't want any more trouble, so, like I said earlier, five or six of us ganged up on him and, after an interesting skirmish, got him down and stomped him. He made the rest of the trip in the sick bay, but there wasn't anything done about it officially.

"Our morale was shot, though. You know, soldiers generally try to keep themselves as neat as they can under any kind of conditions, but we didn't. We just let everything go to hell. When we got to Tientsin we were the most beaten-up, beaten-out looking gang of hoodlums you could imagine. Our uniforms were torn; we needed shaves and haircuts. We knew how lousy we looked, and we just felt like hell. We *were* the scum of the earth, and no mistake. That black book against us had gone on ahead of us to Tientsin, and that didn't make us feel any better either. They marched us around the Compound—like they always do—when we got here, and nobody said a word. Then they halted us, and we formed in a kind of protective mob, and the regimental commander came right up to us. We gritted our teeth and got ready for another bawling out from top to bottom.

"He's gone now, of course, and neither of you guys ever saw him. He was a lieutenant colonel, and his name was George Catlett Marshall. He looked us over for a minute or two, and then he said, 'From what I've been able to gather, you men have had an unusual trip over here. I never make any threats, but if any of you think you're tough, you'll probably find somebody as tough or tougher here than you are. The main thing that I want to say to you now is that when you walked through that gate five minutes ago—the gate of the United States Army Forces Compound in Tientsin, China—the old book was thrown away, and the new book was opened. That new book is yours. I hope you keep the pages of it clean.' Then *he* saluted *us* and walked away. He was a good guy."

Here, as happens to all storytellers, Pfc. Robert Counts ran out of wind and paused to drink some beer. "Man, that seems like a long time ago," he said as he put his glass down.

"Yeah," said little Shaw, "but what happened to that there Alaska Canning, the guy you claim caused all the trouble?"

"Well," said Counts, "old Alaska just didn't seem to belong somehow. He slugged an officer one day. They—uh—punished him and then checked him over and sent him home on a goofy discharge."

"I still don't think he could of beat Reeves," said Shaw.

"Yes, he could of, kid," said Counts. "He was a mighty good fighter—that is, he was before we stomped his face in that time off Luzon."

THE STREETS

2 ❋

When recruits arrived in Tientsin as replacements for
departed 15th infantrymen, they had to stay in the Compound until the first phases of their recruit training were
finished and until their uniforms had been tailored for and
delivered to them. These necessities were synchronized nicely
and probably deliberately. Military bearing and deportment
had to be instilled in a man before he could be judged worthy
to be turned loose on the streets, and, as a concomitant, he
had to be properly dressed. The uniforms they had issued
us back in the States when we had enlisted were First World
War leftovers and could hardly be called proper dress for
scarecrows.

With the achievement of military bearing and nicely fitting
uniforms came the issuance of red passes. These allowed
one to quit the Compound any time one wasn't on duty, and
only required one to be back by midnight when Taps was

blown and bedcheck taken. After six months, if we had behaved ourselves, blue passes would be issued. These allowed one to stay out all night, and only required one to be back in time for roll call at Reveille.

During recruit training we had been taken for short marches around the area of Tientsin in the immediate neighborhood of the Compound, and this had served to whet our desires to see more of the mysterious, smelly city. It was late in the spring of 1927 on a warm Saturday that we received our Hong Kong khaki uniforms, our red passes, and the admonition, if we did leave the Compound, to behave ourselves and not get into any trouble on our first day of freedom. I had a ten-dollar bill, a gift from home. Martin Lord was waiting for me in the dayroom. He had enlisted on the same day as I had back in Fort Leavenworth; we both came from small Midwestern towns and had much in common, except that Lord was far more imbued with the martial spirit than I. He was killed in the Philippines—bearing the rank of captain—soon after America's entry in the Second World War.

We walked across the parade ground. It was thronged with other soldiers, dressed as we were in golden Hong Kong khaki, buttons shining, leather gleaming. Our lapel ornaments were little blue and white shields bearing four acorns, a rampant dragon, and the motto "Can Do." The dragon represented service in China; the four acorns stood for Murfreesboro, Chickamauga, Chattanooga, and Atlanta.

Martin Lord and I walked out the main gate, full of military bearing, our red passes in our breast pockets, swagger sticks under our arms.

The street which led immediately away from the Compound's main gate was lined on the right-hand side with two-story buildings, on the left with one-story shops. The first shop displayed a large sign which said:

> Yung Shing Hau
> Money Exchanger
> General Storekeeper, Provisions
> Wine & Spirits Merchants

Across the street was another shop with an equally big sign which said:

> Shing Chee & Co., Inc.
> Money Exchanger
> General Storekeeper
> Wine & Spirits Goods

Down the street hung more signs:

> Gloria Bar
> Welcome Bar
> Green Parrot Bar

The signs saying "Bar" seemed to stretch into infinity.

There were no sidewalks; one walked in the street itself. Little culverts led from the street across the deep, open gutters to the doors of the shops. These gutters, the city's only sanitary system except for the cesspools in the compounds, were the major sources of Tientsin's smell.

Martin Lord and I went into Shing Chee & Co., Inc., to exchange my ten-dollar bill for Chinese money. We received three dollars and seventy-nine cents for each American dollar. Had my bill been a gold piece, we would have got three dollars and eighty cents. The money was in pretty little bills printed by the Yokohama Specie Bank. The big foreign banks in Tientsin issued their own paper money in those days; their currency was accepted at face value anywhere; that of the Chinese banks never was.

The street was jammed with soldiers afoot, jinrikisha

boys yelling for customers, and beggars pleading for cum-shaw. Lord and I walked away from the squalid environs, seeking the greater glories of the city, commenting contemptuously on how the scum and sweepings always congregated around the gates of an army.

When we came to Woodrow Wilson Street we saw our first automobile, a brown Cadillac sedan, high and stately, moving at a speed of almost seven miles an hour among the donkey carts, jinrikishas, burden carriers, and wheelbarrow pushers. On its radiator was a big red star. We knew what that meant. We stopped, stood at attention, and saluted smartly as the Cadillac chugged past. In it, Brigadier General Joseph Castner leaned forward from the back seat, looked us over, and returned our salute. He was the commanding officer of the United States Army Forces in China. If we had not noticed the Cadillac and had failed to salute, he would have ordered his chauffeur to wheel the car around, would have halted us with a bellow, taken our names, and ordered us back to the Compound under arrest. He never accepted any excuses—even from a commissioned officer—for not being seen and saluted.

Woodrow Wilson Street was bordered with broad, tree-lined sidewalks. The architecture was gray and massive and reflected the tastes of the Germans who had been masters there before the First World War. Castner's Cadillac was the only motor vehicle we saw. Everything else was either animal-drawn or man-drawn. A funeral procession, like a long, gaudy, noisy worm, wriggled its way through everything. An important man was being put to rest; his catafalque was enormous and was borne on the shoulders of fifty men. The hired mourners numbered more than a hundred. There were flute players and string players and gong beaters galore. The music wailed, the mourners mourned, the banners and standards fluttered, the great catafalque swayed and creaked on the shoulders of its bearers. Nobody paid any attention at all except Martin Lord and myself.

A group of Japanese officers came along on the most beautiful horses I had ever seen. Tiny bespectacled men in neat brown uniforms, high leather boots, golden braid on their shoulders, sabers at their waists, they rode their beautiful horses right through the funeral procession, and no one paid any attention to that, either. "What a hell of a country," said Martin Lord.

We walked on and gave way for a platoon of Chinese policemen led by a towering Sikh sergeant, turbaned, bearded, and snappy. The policemen wore big Mauser pistols at their Sam Browne belts, were uniformed in green with black spiral puttees, wore caps like streetcar conductors, and were shod with black slippers. The Sikh sergeant saluted us; we hesitated a second, then saluted him back.

A company of Annamite soldiers from the French garrison, led by a young French officer, came along on a march. They wore spiked, funnel-shaped hats, and carried little carbines. "Let's give 'em a salute," said Lord. "This is getting to be fun." We did so. The officer called his command to attention and saluted us back. "Remember how it was in Leavenworth?" asked Lord. "Where a soldier was a kind of a bum?"

The street signs changed from "Woodrow Wilson" to the Victoria Road label, and we knew we were in the British Concession. Rather soon we were in the very heart of it, in Victoria Park across the street from the Victoria Hotel and in the shadow of Gordon Hall. Chinese gardeners were changing the flowers in the plots. The park's main feature was a circular walk lined with benches, and we sat down to watch the people of the British Concession take their Saturday afternoon strolls. They were a heterogeneous people. Many, of course, were Chinese, gowned and slippered, walking gravely. They wore skullcaps. Sometimes they led police dogs or chows on leashes. These were the patrician Chinese, and their muted, expensive garb became them strangely, even in this setting which was not Chinese at all, but Victorian England. The Eurasians wore European clothing. Many of their women were beautiful, and their spring dress was exquisite. It was the white civilians in that lovely park who looked out of place. The soldiers—15th infantrymen and Welsh Borderers—did not. Their tunics somehow fitted in. It was very quiet there. People strolled about or sat on benches and watched the strollers. There were no vendors or beggars in Victoria Park, although otherwise the streets of Tientsin were crawling with them.

One young girl, walking unaccompanied, attracted the eyes of Martin Lord and myself. She wore a flowered frock which, in the style of those days, reached only to her knees. She wore white gloves and a flowered hat. Her tan silk stockings were rolled to just beneath her knees. As she walked, so lovely, so young, so pensive, and so alone, one's eyes took in her grace, her features, and then settled on those provocative knees. She looked like an American schoolgirl, but not exactly so. Later, we asked the old-timers at our barracks about her. Sure, they had seen her—many times. But she wasn't an American schoolgirl by any means. She was part German, part Russian, part Chinese, and was the concubine of a Japanese banker.

We left the park and walked on, and presently Victoria Road became Rue de France; and Rue de France presently gave way to Via Italia; and the streets were lined with bulky, ugly, monstrous piles of buildings, as if we were in some hideous business section of Europe. Here we saw our first Italian counterparts. They were marines and were dressed in green army-type breeches with green spiral puttees, green porkpie sailor hats, and green sailor shirts. They were arguing over a bottle of wine one of them carried; they laughed at us good-naturedly. One of them started to sing. It was *Giovinezza*, Mussolini's great marching song. And then we came upon the river, the Hai Ho. A Japanese destroyer was tied up at the Bund. A Norwegian freighter was in the swinging berth, warping itself around. Tugs towed strings of lighters. Junks and sampans were towed by coolies on the towpaths or poled by coolies on the poling decks. Out in a clear stretch of water we saw what appeared to be a giant water bug, straddling itself along. It was a Britisher having a river outing in his single scull. Long threads of coolies were unloading sacks of flour from a barge. As do leaf-carrying ants, each picked up, shouldered, and walked off with his sack of flour, and the long line of them disappeared down a walled street to some godown where the flour would be stored. Everybody sang. Everybody toiled, except the Britisher idling in his single scull and the two American soldiers standing, looking, on the Bund.

We went on up along the Bund, and watched the bore come up the teeming river, a lapping, surging, steadily rising wave which had made the seventy-mile journey up the Hai Ho from its birthplace at Taku Bar, and which, as soon as it spent itself, would ebb back down the Hai Ho to Taku Bar again. Day and night, the river rose and fell.

We wandered off into side streets where everything was walled. Godowns, compounds, yamens all had their own walls. The roofs rearing up behind the walls were of tile, and they sloped and bore gargoyles on their ridges and eaves. There were gates in the yamen walls, some of the gates being houses in themselves; and all the gates were guarded by men with guns. The mandarins lived here.

We had strayed too far and didn't know where we were any more. We were getting hungry and knew we would be too late for supper at the barracks. Well, we had anticipated all this, and were prepared. We stood on a street corner, and waved and waited. Five jinrikishas converged

upon us, as beasts converge upon thrown-out scraps of food.
We boarded the first ones to reach us and recited the magic
incantation "*Mei kuo ying p'an*"—American Compound—
which every jinrikisha coolie in Tientsin understood as long
as the giver thereof was in the U. S. Army uniform.

This was our maiden jinrikisha ride. It never occurred
to us then, or during the remainder of our tour in North
China, that it would some day be denounced as degrading to
allow oneself to be towed through the streets by another
human being, towed like a pagan lord who had no regard
for the dignity of his fellow man's soul. It seemed to us
then as being a mighty pleasant, mighty appropriate way of
riding in Tientsin, and our jinrikisha pullers seemed mighty
happy over their fares. Jinrikishas on macadamized streets
are the most comfortable form of transportation ever devised; as might princes in palanquins, but with far less jostling,
we rode down Via Italia, Rue de France, Victoria Road; and
then, by hand-wavings and directional gestures, drew up at
the steps of the Hotel du Nord.

Of the Du Nord we knew nothing except that it was a
hotel, and in the country from which we came hotels served
food. We went up the steps and went in. A Chinese in white
looked at us questioningly. I said, "Dinner." He led us
to a draped dining booth. Martin Lord said, "*Vin blanc.*"
The white-robed Chinese nodded and left. Around us in
other booths sat other diners, all Europeans. They showed
no surprise at all at our entry.

A waiter brought us a bottle, a tall, thin bottle, labeled
Liebfraumilch. Martin Lord and I looked at each other. "How
come?" I asked. "Well," said Lord, "I tried out my French
and asked for white wine, and we get this German stuff. I
guess it's all right." He waved his hand at the waiter. "Pour,
please," he said. The waiter bowed, uncorked the Liebfraumilch, and poured us each a glass. "To Tientsin," said Lord.
My previous experiences with wine had been limited to

home-fermented elderberry at a neighbor's back in Missouri and some smuggled-in Dago Red while on Angel Island in San Francisco Bay. The first taste of this Liebfraumilch, then, was a landmark. There may be finer wines. . . .

We were served a soup, light and hot and with little green petals in it. A loaf of French bread was at hand as was a huge pot of tea. Then came veal cutlets, thin as blintzes, in a subtle sauce and accompanied by tiny potato puff balls. Then came duck, cooked in what manner I do not know, except that later I found that the Hotel du Nord was famed for it. Then came ham and some sort of melon. Then came a crisp white fish and a sauce that was made in heaven. Then came squab and cups of broth and a bowl of rice. We ate it all and washed it down with Liebfraumilch.

"They must think we're major generals," said Lord. "I hope they don't charge us on the same basis." They didn't. The bill was twelve dollars Mex for both of us, or about three and a half dollars American. Still and all, in those days it was one of the most expensive places in Tientsin to eat.

We left the Du Nord and boarded jinrikishas and rode around for an hour or two to digest. Many beggars were still at the Compound gate when we decided to turn in for the night. After paying off the jinrikisha boys, we distributed loose change among the lepers and the cripples, nodded amiably to the scowling Military Police, and strolled across the empty parade ground to our barracks. Taps blew as we mounted the stairs.

BRUCE FERGUSON

3 ❋

When I first arrived in North China, the Coldstream
Guards had left their garrison in the British Concession and
had been replaced by a battalion of the Welsh Border Regiment. As I understand it, the way the British worked it in
those days was to replace battalion for battalion as a unit,
and not keep the same unit forever in one spot as the
Americans did, feeding new men into it as terms of enlistment expired for the old hands. The British kept one battalion
of the Border Regiment, say, in England while the other
battalions served variously in India or Africa or China. The
overseas battalions were commanded by lieutenant colonels;
back in Britain and over everybody was a mysterious colo-
nel-commandant who was actually a lieutenant general and
about whom none of the troops knew very much, except
that he did exist. At least, that was all I could gather from
Bruce Ferguson, who came to Tientsin as a private in the

Royal Scots Guards after the Welsh Borderers were sent home.

The Royal Scots were a snappy outfit. Not kilted, they wore dark plaid straight-legged pants and tan tunics and jaunty Glengarry caps. They also wore all kinds of puzzling insignia on their Glengarries, their collars, and their shoulders. I met Ferguson one day when I was in Victoria Park. He was lounging on the steps of Gordon Hall, shining in his Royal Scots finery, and I, in the equal finery of the 15th Infantry winter O.D.s, was sitting on a bench nearby. I was smoking an obviously American cigarette. (They cost six cents a pack in our canteen: no tax.) Ferguson got up, made a tour or two of the park's garden plots, then came up to me diffidently and said, "Aye, chap, could you let a fellow have one of them smokes? Ah forgot to bring any along."

He was younger than I was, and much newer to China, and I felt companionable. I offered him my pack. He sat down and we began to talk, and soon we were hitting it off quite well, although his accent was hard to understand, and many of the words I used were incomprehensible to him. He had enlisted about six months before—it was all a young chap could do in Glasgow in those days except work in the bloody shops—and had received his recruit training at some place—he didn't know exactly where. I had been thinking of rabbit hunting back in Missouri when he stopped to bum me for a cigarette and, after a while, I got around to asking him if he had ever gone rabbit hunting back in Scotland. He didn't even know what a rabbit was. I described the rodent to him minutely and with gestures. "Ah," he said, "you're pullin' mah leg. You meant hare all the time."

"Yes," I said, "I did. And many's the great hare hunts we had back in Missouri. Didn't you ever hunt hare in Scotland?"

No, he said. Hunting was for the poaching chaps and the lairds, not for a bloody working chap like him. I remarked that young cottontail hare were uncommonly good eating.

He didn't know about that, but he twirled his swagger stick for a while and then said, "They tell me you Yanks eats fit for kings in yer mess."

"We do all right," I said, twirling my swagger stick. "Of course, though, the table our mess sergeant sets for us wouldn't compare to the average Missouri farmer's meal. But food's so cheap here in China that we manage quite well."

"This Messoori yuh keep jawin' aboot," he said. "That ayn't that hellhole in India, is it?"

"No, no," I said. "It's one of the forty-eight United States. Right in the middle of them, in fact. Many of the people are farmers."

He thought that over for a while and then said, "I didn't think you Yanks did service in India." And then: "Farmer folk in Scotland eats very poor."

"Is that why so many of them join the British Army?" I asked.

"The British Army feeds poorest of all," said Ferguson. "Domn poor. That'd be no reason for joinin'."

"Oh, it can't be as bad as all that," I said. "What, for instance, did you have today?"

"Puddin'," he said. "A stinkin' puddin'. There'll be more of it tonight. Ah hates it."

Then, apparently to change the subject, he asked, "How many pockets you got in them breeks of yours?"

"Five," I said, indicating the two front pockets, the two hip pockets, and the watch pocket of my slacks. "Why?"

"They only allow us one," he said. "So we can't stuff our bloody hands in 'em all the time like you chaps do. This'n." And he showed me the little fob in the waistband of his plaids. "Every 'ore in London knows where it is, though." He drew from it a two-dollar Chinese bill. "Ah'll stand yuh for a beer," he said.

"A beer would be fine," I said. "Where shall we go?"

"Ah don't care. Some place near yer barracks, though. Ah don't like it none 'ere."

So we went to the Green Parrot, which was on the street leading to the American Compound and was presided over by a White Russian lady boniface named Fanya. The Parrot was popular with the 15th infantrymen because Fanya, after she came to know you and your drinking habits, would allow credit on the last few days before payday. There were no American-type bars as such in Tientsin in those days. There was no rail at which to stand and there was no beer on tap. You sat at tables, and a blue-robed Chinese boy waited on you, and your beer was poured from bottles into glasses.

Ferguson asked me what I would have, and I ordered Kupper, which was made in Munich and was one of the world's great beers. "Ah'll have the same," he said. Poor chap, the only beer he'd had in China before that had been the tepid brew they served in the British canteen. The two tall bottles of Kupper wiped out most of his poor little two-dollar bill of Chinese money, and it was with a pang that I realized I had nearly beggared him with one quaff. But he didn't wince or complain. He only remarked that the price of beer near our Compound was much more dear than one would expect. "Places in London cheats soldier chaps, too," he said.

There was nothing for it but for me to buy him a beer in return and, of course, another for myself. As we were downing them, he said, "They tell me sometimes you chaps invites some of our chaps to yer mess for a meal."

"Oh, yes," I said. "It's simple enough. All we have to do is ask the mess sergeant an hour or two before chow call, and he has the mess coolies set out an extra plate."

Then I saw what he was driving at and how he had

trapped me into it. "Would you," I asked, trying not to sound sarcastic, "like to be the guest of Company E of the 15th Infantry at supper tonight? All we're having is fried ham and potatoes and biscuits and things like that, but you're welcome."

"Yes," he said. "Ah wud. Thankee."

So I took my Royal Scot to our barracks and introduced him to Mess Sergeant Anton Frerichs and asked if it would be all right to have him for my supper guest that evening. "Okay, but don't make no habit of it," said Sergeant Frerichs.

It was still an hour to supper, so I took Ferguson to the dayroom and asked him if he would like to play a game of checkers. He didn't know what checkers meant; I showed him the board and the counters. "Ah," he said, "pullin' mah leg again. You mean draughts. Aye, I'll play ye a game." We played, and I beat him easily, because I had been tutoring under the company barber, who was an acknowledged grand master of the art.

Other members of the company drifted in and out of the dayroom, waiting for chow call. They looked incuriously at the Royal Scot, for frequently we had men from the other garrisons in to eat with us. In fact, little Calhoun Shaw soon appeared with a young Italian marine in tow. When Shaw asked Sergeant Frerichs if the Italian could share the mess also, Frerichs let out a bellow to the effect that he, Frerichs, hadn't signed on to feed the Foreign Legion; but when he saw the hurt look on Shaw's face, he relented and said, "Okay, but don't make no habit of it. And I mean it this time."

The young Italian spoke no English, nor Shaw any Italian. They conversed entirely by means of giggles and gestures and grunts and had a wonderful time of it. Some of the other men made bets on which would eat the most— my Scottie or Shaw's Wop.

It turned out they both ate about the same amount—something like twice as much as any of the heaviest feeders of the company could put down that night. Hot biscuits and ham gravy seemed to be their particular delight, but they didn't altogether ignore the ham, either.

I offered to pay Ferguson's jinrikisha fare back to his barracks that night, but he said he'd rather walk; he needed to shake down the food he had eaten. I said, "You should try our mess when we have something that's *really* good."

"Ah will," he said. "Ah can come any time. Thankee, chap."

By any time, he apparently meant every day, for every afternoon except those in which he was on guard, he turned up. After the third time, Mess Sergeant Frerichs put his foot down hard; and it was my unpleasant duty to tell Ferguson that he had worn out his welcome. He took it bitterly but philosophically. "All sergeants," said he, "is bahstards, Scottish and Yank alike. Ah'll meet ye in the park again sometime, chap, and we'll have another good talk and a stroll."

Once, at a previous meeting, I had asked him about the insigne of strange device which the Royal Scots Guards wore on their Glengarries. "It's nuthin'," he said. "Pontius Pilate's Scots Guards is what it means. But it's nuthin'."

"Pontius Pilate?" I said. "He wasn't in Scotland."

"Ah never said 'e was. We was with 'im. It's all in our book. Ah ayn't read it all, but ah'll bring you the book and you can read it."

So, once when we met in Victoria Park, he brought along the little regimental book which was given to each Royal Scot at the time of his enlistment. It was about the shape and size of the Stedman Missal. It contained the history of the regiment and a list of the battles in which the regiment had been engaged. I read it over a bottle of Château la Rose in the Café Genève; history swirled up around me in smoke and flame.

The Royal Scots, their regimental legend claimed, formed the oldest continuous military organization on earth. Julius Caesar, when he conquered Britain, had run constantly afoul of the Scots and, being unable to do anything else with them, formed them into a legion of their own, officered them with Romans, and sent them packing to duty hither and yon throughout the Roman Empire. They were too wild for Rome itself and too wild for other of the big Mediterranean cities, so they were sent to the Middle East to do garrison duty in Palestine. Regimes changed in Rome and emperors came and went; eventually a man named Pontius Pilate was named procurator of Judea, and the Scots were assigned to him as his own troops. They thereupon became known as Pontius Pilate's Scots Guards and wore a distinctive insigne, apparently almost exactly like the one Bruce Ferguson and his mates still wore on their Glengarries. By then, they had adopted Romanized names, but they were still Scots through and through and replacements for their legion came from Scotland.

The Jews became strangely restive, and Pilate's Guards were kept busy. A detail of them arrested a certain Man; and another detail of them drew lots for His clothes; and another detail of them stood watch over His tomb. Well, they were only professional soldiers doing duty in a foreign land.

The empire began to crumble, and the Scots, as did the other legions, fell back and back until they were in Rome itself, fighting against the Goths. They retained their unity; it was already centuries old. When the empire disintegrated, they returned—what was left of them—in a body to Scotland. Here, their history fades for some centuries—the Royal

Scots count centuries as other regiments do years—but they were raised again in Scotland in the 1600s; and, after the Restoration, they were brought under the Crown in 1707 and began their service for British kings and queens.

When I returned the book to Ferguson, I said, "I talked to Sergeant Frerichs, and he said it would be all right for you to eat chow with us Sunday, if you'd like."

"Thankee, chap," he said. "Ah'd be glad to. You Yanks eat like kings, y'know. Like bloody kings off the fat of the land."

SHILOH

4

I lay on my bunk and told Digby Hand of Arkansas about the Royal Scots Guards and their legend. That morning, in a special regimental ceremony, Company E had been awarded the Chickamauga Guidon. A guidon, of course, is a flag carried on a staff at the head of a company. The Chickamauga Guidon flaunted a red acorn on a yellow field; it was awarded yearly to that company of the 15th Infantry which had attained the highest degree of military proficiency according to the regulations established by the regimental commander. It was to be carried in all formations where the regular company guidon itself was carried. Digby Hand, because of his six-foot-two height, had been named to carry the Chickamauga Guidon. During the Civil War, the 15th Infantry, along with other regiments under General Thomas, had earned for itself the title "Rock of Chickamauga" when it stood fast against the assaults of Braxton Bragg's men.

Short-timer, our squad boy, had just brought us canteens of previously boiled but now ice-cold water, and, having done that, was sitting on the squadroom floor, polishing our shoes and the buttons of our blouses. "Run over to the canteen, Short-timer," said Digby Hand, "and get me some chewing tobaccer. Damn if I ain't just fresh out." Short-timer put away his polishing kit and trotted off.

I lay on my bunk, thinking of Pontius Pilate's Scots Guards at the Tomb of Christ and the 15th infantrymen at Chickamauga under old Pap Thomas, and how it seemed so silly that we should all be here together in Tientsin, piddling around. I asked Digby Hand of Arkansas if he put much stock in army traditions and army legends and army boasting and whatnot. Or did he think it all baloney?

"No," he said. "I think it's true. You cain't have a legend without having had something happen some time. It was on account of a story about the 15th Infantry that I up and joined it. My grandpaw told me the story. He's ninety-four now, a great one for talking. I don't reckon he's shut his mouth—'cept when he's sleeping—for the last forty years of his life. He was in the Civil War, you know, and he told me about the 15th; that's why I up and joined it."

"Good Lord," I said. "Did your grandpaw fight in *this* outfit in the Civil War?"

"Fight *in it?*" sniffed Hand. "Course not! He fought *agin'* it. Under Forrest. Mr. Nathan Bedford Forrest. He was a general, but everybody called him mister. At least, that's what Grandpaw claims."

"I've read about him," I said.

"Well, I *heard* about him," said Hand. "Every day, seems like, for going on twenty years till I up and joined the army. I got it poured into me 'cause I had to kind of help look out for Grandpaw, and looking out for him meant listening to him.

"He and Forrest were neighbors when the war broke out. After the war, Grandpaw moved to Arkansas where I was born. Forrest was forty-two years old and over six foot tall and a millionaire and left-handed. He up and enlisted as a private. Grandpaw was only in his twenties at the time, and he looked up to Mr. Forrest a whole hell of a lot.

"Forrest never stayed a private long enough to learn how to salute. They made him a colonel and told him to go out and recruit himself a regiment and use his own money doing it. He saw Grandpaw sitting on a fence rail one morning, and he said, 'Hey, there, young fella, I'm looking for a pack of devils forty times meaner than myself. You wanta come along?' And Grandpaw said, 'Yessir, Mr. Forrest, I reckon I do.' And that was how he come to join the Confederate army. Forrest was recruiting cavalry, so Grandpaw had to take along a horse; and Forrest didn't have any guns to pass around, so Grandpaw had to take along his daddy's deer rifle. And Forrest didn't have any uniforms to hand out, so Grandpaw just went along as he was. Generally after that, though, he wore Federal uniforms taken off Union soldiers. They were made better than Confederate stuff and a lot easier to come by.

"Forrest didn't have any military training, and he made up

his own rules as he went along. When he yelled at his command, 'Scatter out, you mudsills!' they knew he meant for 'em to deploy as skirmishers; and when he yelled, 'Herd up tight ag'in!' they knew he meant for 'em to form in a column of twos. And, of course, when he yelled 'Charge!' there was never any question about what he meant.

"Well, they fought first at Donelson, and the two Southern generals there couldn't get together on anything, least of all on how to fight their troops, so both of 'em ended by surrendering to Grant. Forrest was boiling mad, Grandpaw said, but they outranked him and told him to shut up and get out. They were West Pointers, too, those generals that surrendered, and Forrest couldn't hardly read or write.

"Well, the next time they fought was at Shiloh, and this time both Grandpaw and Forrest figured they'd get something done because Albert Sidney Johnston was bossing the Rebs, and, although he was a West Pointer, too, everybody —even Grandpaw—thought he was a good general. So what does Albert Sidney Johnston do? 'Why,' says Grandpaw, 'he gits himself kilt the very first day when we was piling into Grant, and there we was under Beauregard!' You should hear Grandpaw say that to really appreciate it.

"Anyhow, the Confederates drove the Yankees back and it looked like they were going to win themselves a battle. But then Buell came up with a half-million more Yanks, and they rallied and beat the tar and daylights out of the Rebs.

"Well, Grandpaw was riding night and day with Forrest, charging here and covering flanks there, and generally having the time of his life. After Buell came up, but before the Rebs were finally licked, there was a pocket out ahead of Grant's lines which the South wanted cleared, and Beauregard called on Forrest to clear it. 'P'int it out to me and consider it done,' says Forrest, and he whistled up Grandpaw and the rest of his gang and pointed with his saber and led off the charge. The Yanks in that particular pocket were well dug in. Mr. Forrest got his horse shot out from under him before he'd gone forty yards. So did a lot of others, including Grandpaw. When the Yanks took aim they meant business and they did business. 'This ain't gettin' us nowhar,' says Forrest. 'All you mudsills git offen your hosses. This is a job we got to do on foot.'

"So, Grandpaw said, Forrest's command dismounted, and they formed a big half-circle, and one end of the circle would move toward the pocket while the other end of the circle fired volleys to make the Yanks keep their heads down. Well, the Yanks never pulled their heads so far but what they couldn't shoot back, and when Forrest finally overran them, he, Forrest, found that he'd lost four men to every Yank in that pocket that he'd killed or captured.

"There weren't any officers or non-coms left among the bluecoats, just privates—young fellows. And there hadn't been very many men in the pocket in the first place—maybe just a platoon. Forrest questioned them after he herded them back through the Confederate lines. 'Who are you young devils, anyway?' he bellowed at them. 'What-all you want to fight so damn hard for?'

"'We're 15th infantrymen,' they told him. 'Fightin's our business.'

"'Well, it's mine, too,' said Forrest. 'I reckon if I run into your kind ag'in in this here war, there won't be many left to tell about it.'

"Well, it wasn't Forrest—it was some other general— that ran into the 15th at Chickamauga, but like Forrest had said there wasn't many left to tell about it."

Short-timer, our squad boy, came back from the canteen and gave Hand his plug of tobacco. "Thanks, Short-timer," said Hand. "Just put it on the book and I'll settle with you on payday." He cut himself off a chew.

"That's the way Grandpaw told it," he said. "I don't know

whether it's legend or not. But when I went to enlist, Grandpaw said—he was ninety-one years old then—'There hain't but one Yankee outfit in this whole world I'd let a grandson of mine jine with, and that's the 15th Infantry. You jine that outfit, my boy, and I'll be proud of you.'"

THE FOOT CAVALRY

5

Our captain had a bad knee—some sort of twist—so on that morning he did not go along on our hike. Our first lieutenant was in the hospital at the time, recovering from an operation, and he could not go. Therefore, our unit, E Company, was commanded by Second Lieutenant Curtis, who was older than either of the two senior officers but, unlike them, was not a West Pointer.

Reveille sounded that morning at three o'clock. Breakfast was served at three-twenty. In our company mess, we had sausage, soft-boiled eggs, hot cakes, and coffee. The way you handled that combination was to make a sort of sandwich on your plate of hot cakes and sausage, and then break soft-boiled eggs over it. I remember using nine eggs —little eggs from little Chinese chickens. It was dark as midnight at ten to four, when we fell in by companies in front of our barracks, carrying full packs as well as rifles and bayonets but no ammunition—a load of about forty pounds. We wore olive-drab shirts and breeches, spiral wool puttees, and campaign hats. The night before, E Company had been admonished by its first sergeant to get to bed early, but in my squad two men had disregarded him and had gone out and got very drunk. One was Borischak, recently broken from the rank of duty sergeant. The other was Robert Counts, recently promoted to the rank of first-class private. The one had been mourning, the other celebrating. Both had such fearful hangovers they hadn't been able to drink their coffee, much less eat sausage, hot cakes, and soft-boiled eggs. We helped them get their packs on and steadied them as we fell in.

"Where we going?" Counts kept asking. "Hell, fellas, I just barely got to bed."

Borischak announced he was too sick to operate and was going back to his bunk. "They got my stripes. What else they want?" he asked.

"It's just a little bye-bye," I assured them as we held them in their places. "You guys can make it. You'll feel better after the first nineteen miles. You'll be kind of numb by then."

Each man was issued a ration of one sandwich, and then Lieutenant Curtis, flashlight in hand, walked along our ranks for a brief inspection. He looked at Counts and Borischak as he passed, but he said nothing. A minute later, though, the first sergeant came up to them and said, "I can't do anything about it now, because we've got to move out at full strength, but man, oh, man, if either of you bozos try to ditch, I'm going to ride you out of the army. And don't forget it."

The hike would be led by Brigadier General Joseph Castner himself. The Third Battalion would follow him and his two aides. Then the colonel and his staff were to fall in, along with Headquarters Company and the Medical and Quartermaster Corps men. The Second Battalion was to bring up the rear. That was all there was then to the American Army in China. The First Battalion was stationed in the Philippines. For several days we had known that this hike was scheduled, but we knew nothing of its projected length. We had been practicing extended marches for a couple of months, starting at ten miles and working up to fifteen, seventeen, and twenty. Counts and Borischak and I were in the last squad of E Company, which was at the tail end of the line of march. At General Castner's signal, the officers gave commands and the regiment started moving out, company falling in behind company, the men at right shoulder arms, marching as trimly as on formal parade.

It was four o'clock and still dark, except for the street lights of Tientsin, but there were throngs of Chinese along the streets to watch us, throngs of silent yellow men in slippers, robes, and skullcaps. They stood and looked without amazement as the 15th U. S. Infantry uncoiled itself down the cool macadamized road that led between the great walled mansions of the city. We kept at right shoulder arms for fifteen minutes. Then the cry "Route order!" came down the line. We slung our rifles from our shoulders, lighted cigarettes, began to chat and gripe, and gradually fell out of step.

"I should of ate some breakfast," said Counts. "I got a hunch Old Joe is gonna hike us clear to hell and gone today."

A column of infantry companies marching at route step is like a long snake, the head of it continually probing forward and the body undulating in rhythmic ripples. At the tail, E Company constantly fell behind, and as the command was relayed down the column "Close up, close up!" we again and again had to break into double time in order to regain our position.

"Goddlemighty," complained Counts. "Are we going to have to keep this up all day? What's Old Joe trying to do, kill us off?"

When we broke into double time, our packs would bounce, the mess-kit compartments would rattle, our rifles would flop and swing, and our feet would pound. This delighted the Chinese along the streets, and they would laugh and shout. Some of them, indeed, themselves danced up and down in pleased mimicry of our dogtrotting.

General Castner planned to take his brown snake, numbering nine hundred men, out of Tientsin and into the open country by the most direct route, but to do this he had to pass through the Market Center, on the edge of the city. At the Market Center were gathered that morning, even though it was not yet full daylight, what seemed to be all the donkey carts of Hopei Province. They were piled with cabbages, kale, onions, melons, squash, chickens, ducks, garlic, and other local produce. Under the high, flaring lamps that illuminated the market street, the produce growers were haggling with the buyers, and everywhere there was bickering and confusion and yelling and jostling. The street itself was jammed. Right through it all General Castner steered his column of infantry—four men abreast—amid the protests and the curses of the Chinese.

By the time E Company had reached the Market Center, we had fallen behind again, and again the command came down, "Close up, E Company! Close up on the ranks ahead." Lieutenant Curtis barked out, "E Company! Double time! March!" We broke into a shuffling trot, and the Chinese stopped their chaffering and howled with laughter as seventy young men pounded their feet in the dust. The Market

Center dogs—scores of them—thought it great fun, too. They yelped and ran alongside us. But one made a mistake and came too close. Ex-Duty Sergeant Borischak, his face drawn with the pain of his hangover, lashed out with his right foot like a quick-kicking quarterback, caught the dog under the chin, and booted it over on its back. Now some of our men laughed and cheered, but our first sergeant put a stop to this with a bitter snarl.

We took our first break of the morning at five o'clock, two miles out of town on the road to Hwei Dui and three and a half miles from our starting point, at the Compound. We weren't even beginning to get tired. Few of us bothered to sit down. Counts ate some of his sandwich and remarked disparagingly on its taste, but said a man had to keep up his strength.

Lieutenant Curtis lectured Borischak about kicking the dog. "You could have started a riot, you know. The Chinese are touchy about their dogs. It was a damfool thing to do."

"Yessir," said Borischak.

Then down the line came the command "Fall in!" and, in a moment, "Route step. March!" and Castner's brown snake was awrithe again.

The road to the town of Hwei Dui, which was seven miles from Tientsin, was a deeply rutted path across the plain. It was broad daylight now, and we marched beside the road instead of upon it, because the footing was better and also because there was much donkey-cart and jinrikisha traffic on the road itself. From somewhere behind us came two sprinting Chinese. One was an old man in a blue gown. Behind him was a boy who carried a bamboo pole across his shoulders with a big basket swinging from each end. In these baskets were peanuts and soda pop. The pair caught up with us, and although we were then marching at almost four miles an hour, the old man trotted along beside us and offered us his wares, imploring us to see how nicely chilled the soda pop was, how delicately roasted were the peanuts. "Gimme some of that strawberry," ordered Borischak. And the old man picked a bottle from the carrier boy's basket, opened it, made change for Borischak, shuffled along patiently until Borischak had done drinking, returned the empty bottle and the salvaged cap to the basket, and then speeded up his carrier so that he could peddle his wares to the company ahead. He was still selling when the column reached Hwei Dui.

We arrived at that village about six o'clock, and the order came to halt and fall out for ten minutes. Hwei Dui was a mud-walled, mud-hut town of a couple of hundred people and pigs and dogs. No tree, no blade of grass grew anywhere around. What the people of Hwei Dui did for a living I could never ascertain. "Stay along the road," came the order down the column. "Keep to hell out of Hwei Dui itself." "Who the hell wants to go into Hwei Dui?" Counts asked as we broke ranks.

The head of the column was actually quite a way beyond Hwei Dui when we halted, and E Company, the tail-end company, was at Hwei Dui's very walls. The Chinese elders came out of the gate and looked. Everywhere they saw olive-drab soldiers with packs and rifles on their backs. The elders bowed and smiled and asked us if we would like benches to sit on. Lieutenant Curtis thanked them gravely, but said no. We would be moving out shortly, he explained. Then the children and the dogs and the pigs of Hwei Dui came forth. The children were wary, the dogs suspicious, the pigs indifferent. The eight of us in my squad sat against the wall of Hwei Dui with legs outstretched, our packs and rifles unslung beside us. A little girl, possibly three or four, came up with her larger companions to examine us at close range.

"Just like looking at bears in the zoo," Counts commented.

One of our squadmates—Digby Hand, from Arkansas—had an idea. "Bears is right," he said. "I think I'll show 'em what bears do." He was six feet two inches tall, as thin as a rake handle, and had a nose like a snipe's. He sniggled his bayonet out of the scabbard on his pack and affixed it to his Springfield. The little Hwei Dui girl looked on intently a few feet away. "Watch now," said Hand. He unwound suddenly to his towering height, let out a war whoop of what he fancied was Chinese profanity, and pretended to charge the little girl with his bayonet. She screamed and tried to run, but tripped and fell and bloodied her nose. The other children took up her screaming.

Our corporal jerked the rifle away from Hand and shoved him back against the wall. "What the hell possessed you to do a thing like that?" he yelled. And to the rest of us he cried, "Quiet that kid down, for Godsake, or Old Joe himself will be down here to see what she's yelling about!"

I, for one, didn't know how to quiet her. But Borischak knew. He had been in China for seven years. "Give her some chow," he said. "Give her the rest of your sandwich, Counts. That'll shut her up."

"Why me?" asked the perplexed Counts. But the corporal seconded the suggestion, and Counts dug into his pack and took out what was left of his sandwich—a crumbly piece of army bread with a mustardy slice of roast beef adhering to it. He went to the little girl, who was cringing on the ground and screeching at the top of her lungs, and said, "Here, honey, gulp this down. It's good for what ails you."

Her screams stopped. She sat up, accepted the food, and took a tentative bite. She stopped sniveling. The other children came up hungrily. "Take out your sandwich, Hand," said the corporal. "Divvy it up with the kids. You started this—now you can finish it. Hurry up. Here comes the lieutenant."

Curtis and the first sergeant had been up ahead, conferring. Now they came down to us. "What's going on here?" Curtis asked the corporal. "Have your men been bothering these children?"

"No, sir," said the corporal. "Counts offered one of them his sandwich, and the other kids got to fighting over it. That little one fell down and banged her nose, but everything's all right now."

"How come Hand's got his bayonet fixed?" demanded the first sergeant.

"The catch has been sticking," the corporal explained. "He oiled it this morning, and he wanted to see if it worked any better."

"He picked a hell of a place to do it," said the first sergeant.

Lieutenant Curtis said, "Why are you giving your chow away, Counts? Don't you like it?"

"Yessir, I like it," said Counts. "But the kids looked hungry."

"Fall your squad in, Corporal," said the lieutenant. "Stand them at attention until we move out. They're just wasting their rest period this way."

So the corporal fell us in, and we stood at attention, the just and the unjust alike, but before anyone had become really angry at the indignity the break ended and the regiment was on the move again.

Two miles beyond Hwei Dui, the road crossed a canal. The bridge at that point had fallen in, so General Castner led us along the canal bank to the next bridge, a mile farther up. Here he crossed and headed back down for the road we had been on. Thus the regiment, for a few minutes, assumed the shape of a giant hairpin, half of it along one side of the canal, going down to the road, the other half along the other side, going up to the bridge, with those troops crossing the bridge forming the tight curve of the pin. Thus it was, also, that for the first time that morning we of the tail-end squad of the tail-end company saw General Castner face to face. He was only about a hundred feet away, striding toward us along the opposite side of the canal, his two aides dogging behind him.

Castner was an enormous man, big of bone and big of belly. He looked like a fat but very muscular giant towing two pygmies—his aides—behind him. He wore the sloppiest, droopiest campaign hat to be seen in the entire regiment, an unpressed O.D. shirt, khaki breeches faded almost white, spiral puttees, and enlisted men's shoes. From the right side of the leather belt that circled his great belly an army pistol flopped in its holster; from the other side a canteen hung. His other impediment was a canvas musette bag, carried from one shoulder. It was only by the silver stars on his shirt collar that one could tell he was a general. The general was eating a fried chicken leg. He was also consulting his pedometer and his wristwatch. Just before we tail-enders drew opposite to him, a voice from up ahead, from the obscurity of the ranks that had already passed him, growled out mournfully, "Hey, Joe, give us a rest." Laughter followed, the anonymous laughter of many of the nine hundred men. Castner's head jerked to the right, he dropped the chicken leg he was gnawing on, and his eyes swept our ranks.

Counts whispered, "Oh, brother, what now?"

At the moment nothing happened. The general never broke his stride, the head of the column tramped along the canal toward the road, the tail tramped on until it crossed the bridge, and finally the command was in a straight line once more. Then, passing down the line came a rumor: Castner was boiling mad at that crack "Hey, Joe, give us a rest," and at the laughter that had followed it, and he was going to walk us for ten straight miles before he allowed another halt. So, just as the squad I was in had had to stand at attention because of Digby Hand's horseplay with his bayonet at Hwei Dui, it now appeared that the whole regiment would have to grind out ten weary miles without a halt because of some other soldier's tomfoolery.

General Castner, who had a tremendous stride, quickened it until he was going four miles an hour. But the ranks of the men behind him could not all quicken their pace in unison with his, and the regiment stretched out until the inexorable "Close up!" snapped it together again. As usual, we at the tail end had to double time more than anybody else.

"I'm going to write my mama," said Digby Hand, mimicking a child's high-pitched voice, "that old man Joe Castner run me all the way across China without letting me catch my breath."

It was about the seventeen-mile mark that the first man

dropped out and sat beside the road. He would be picked up later by a mule-drawn vehicle known as an escort wagon. A machine-gun company lieutenant, he sat on a dirt mound, and we passed him on the double, for we were closing up again. He had taken off one of his boots and the sock, and there was a big splotch of blood on his heel.

"Nail came through," he explained to Lieutenant Curtis as we trotted by. "Cut clear to the bone."

After that, and for ten unbroken miles, we passed other occasional drop-outs. There didn't seem to be any single cause. Some of the men had bad feet, some had bad legs, some had weak stomachs. We did nothing for them except to jeer at the ones we knew.

Following a circular route, the regiment covered twenty-

five miles in the eight hours we marched that morning. We of E Company, the tail-end company that had spent so much time at a dogtrot catching up, had not lost a man. Old Joe had cracked the whip, but he had not been able to snap us loose. We were angry at him, but we were also proud of ourselves. Castner led us back to the Compound for a mid-day hour-long halt. We then heard that the actual reason for the unbroken ten-mile stretch was to make up time and mileage lost because of the detour at the bridge. He had not been really angered by that crack "Hey, Joe, give us a rest."

In the comfort of our barracks, we soaked our feet, changed shoes and socks, and massaged our thigh muscles, and then ate a dinner of thick soup, steak, mashed potatoes, and ice cream. While we were eating, Lieutenant Curtis appeared. Someone shouted "Attention!" as he came into the mess hall, but Curtis said, "Go on eating." Then he said he had some good news for us. We would be the leadoff company for the afternoon's march. General Castner had taken cognizance of the beating we had endured all morning as tail-enders and had decided to reverse the order for the remainder of the hike. That meant, Curtis pointed out, there would be no more damned double-timing to catch up, for we would be the pace setters. Curtis also said that, except for some needless cavorting in the ranks, he was well pleased with the company's conduct on the march. He said he was proud that E Company had not lost a man, and he felt sure that we would complete the afternoon portion of the hike without doing so, either.

"Can the lieutenant say how far we are going this afternoon?" asked the first sergeant.

"No, the lieutenant can't," replied Curtis. "He's not in the general's confidence. But I'll tell you this—fill your canteens full before you start out."

The dinner and the rest had made new men of Counts and Borischak. They and Digby Hand and I were reclining on our bunks in the squadroom when the first sergeant came in and, without any preface, said, "I told you guys this morning that I was going to ride you out of the army if you tried to ditch on me. You didn't ditch, 'cause you couldn't, but you made me look pretty damn silly between that dog business and those kids at Hwei Dui. The men in every other company, except that knucklehead who yelled at the general, behaved themselves. But oh, no, not the guys in my company. It's got to be guys in my company that horse around with bayonets and kick dogs and scare kids. But I'm first sergeant of this outfit, and what this outfit does reflects on me. I'm not standing any more nonsense. I'm warning you jokers. You pull anything this afternoon and, brother, you're on my list. Just try anything and see." So saying, he left.

"Well," said Counts, "what's eating him?"

Digby Hand whinnied. "Gentlemen," he said, "our first sergeant has been hitting honorable bottle. You can always tell when he tries to talk dignified. And drinking means he's beginning to feel pain. Didja notice the squint in his eye? Lieutenant Curtis said to fill the canteens. Our first sergeant has went and filled his with redeye. I betcha if Old Joe tries to squeeze too many miles out of us this afternoon that our top-kick bastard falls on his face. That man never drinks unless he's in pain."

"Not him," said Borischak. "He'll make it, pain or no pain. He's a bohunk, like me. He's tough."

"I got second sight," persisted Hand. "I bet six beers if anybody falls out of E Company this afternoon it'll be the top kicker."

"I'll take three of those beers," said Counts.

"I'll take the other three," said Borischak. "He'll finish the hike."

Despite such brave talk, all of us were stiff and unhappy when, at the end of the hour, the order came to get off our bunks and move out of our barracks and fall in. There was much grumbling. We had done twenty-five miles. Wasn't that enough for any general in his right mind? There wasn't any war going on. What was the point in hiking us until we fell on our faces?

"That will be enough of that kind of talk," said Lieutenant Curtis. "Fall the company in," he said to the first sergeant, "and let's get to the head of the line."

We marched past the other units to the main gate of the Compound. General Castner and aides, the colonel and his staff, and the battalion commanders were standing there.

"Lose any men, Curtis?" asked a bespectacled lieutenant colonel. (His name was Joseph Stilwell.)

"No, sir," said Curtis.

There was a noticeable change as the other companies fell in behind us. In the early morning, everything had been done with military snap. Now there was a kind of slackness. General Castner looked at his wristwatch and adjusted his pedometer. "Move out your regiment, Colonel," he said, and, motioning to his aides, he started off.

We of E Company followed him at a distance of twenty paces. Behind us, the colonel and his staff fell in, and behind them came the rest of the regiment. The Chinese, more thickly than ever, thronged the sidewalks to watch as, at a listless right shoulder arms, the tired foreign army resumed its march. General Castner chose for his afternoon route an abandoned railroad spur line that led out over the plain in the opposite direction from which we had marched in the morning. The track was laid on a narrow embankment, lined with trees, between flooded paddy fields. It was impossible to walk four abreast on the roadbed. We split into a column of twos, thus stretching the regiment out to twice its former length.

Every outfit except E Company was losing men. They weren't quitters; they were just physically incapable of walking any more for the time being. Notable among them were the number of athletes—basketball players, prizefighters, baseball and handball stars—who heretofore had seemed the epitome of physical fitness. But their strength, apparently, lay in concentrated bursts of energy rather than in endurance. After they had rested sufficiently, they would have to walk back, because the escort wagons couldn't operate along the narrow rail spur.

At the end of the first hour, when we stopped for a ten-minute break, we unslung our packs and, lying down, rested our feet upon them. This was supposed to allow the blood to run out of the feet and thus ease the pain. But the pain was not so much in one's feet any more. It was in the thighs, and it was clear down through the muscle and into the bone. From knee to hip that pain flared; the rest of one's body was numb, even the shoulders, into which the pack straps and the rifle sling had eaten for so long.

We then continued straight along the railroad spur, with never a turn or a twist, until the second hour was up and we took another break. Off came our packs, and down we lay. Fifteen yards ahead of us, General Castner and his aides sat down on the rails. In a kind of disguised stagger, the colonel and his staff officers came up to the general. They took seats opposite him and talked in low tones. We could overhear enough to know that they were trying to get him to call off the hike and go back to the Compound. He said something to the colonel, the colonel nodded in vigorous agreement, and we took a twenty-minute break instead of the usual ten.

At the head of E Company, the first sergeant and Lieutenant Curtis sat side by side on a pile of ties. Twice during that twenty-minute break, I saw the first sergeant drink from his canteen. Curtis looked fit enough still, but the top kick looked exhausted. His eyes had a moist, glazed look, and there was no doubt now that his canteen had whiskey in it.

General Castner spoke to the colonel, and the regiment was ordered to its feet. Then Castner personally gave the order to about-face, waving his hands angrily at us in E Company until we did so. We were stupefied—not only at the thought that we were at last going back but at the unusual order. The order was, of course, the sensible thing to do. Castner couldn't loop his regiment around in the mud paddies, and he couldn't double us back on ourselves along that crowded embankment, so he turned every man around in his tracks. It took a lot of astonished bawlings all the way down the line to do this, but it was done. And there we were in E Company at the tail end of the regiment again, and the ones who formerly had been at the tail end were now at the head and, being at least a mile down the track from us, had that much less distance to walk back to the Compound.

Castner left the colonel and his staff sitting on the rails, soaking up every second of rest that they could. With his aides, the general walked back along the whole length of the reversed regiment and took up his station at its new head. When he passed by me, I swear he looked as rugged as he had that morning along the canal bank, but his aides— young enough to be his sons—looked like men about to die. I have since thought that General Castner didn't need much urging to curtail the march. He had only been waiting, I believe, for his officers to beg him to do so. As the oldest man in the United States Army Forces in China, he had wanted to show them that he was also the toughest.

The order to resume the march came down the line, and we started back to Tientsin—a distance of five and three-quarters miles. Soon we began to pass men who had been unable to continue after the twenty-minute break. They sat limply, but after they had rested some more they, like the

athletes who had dropped out earlier, would have to plod on.
E Company still slogged along intact, and I told Digby Hand
I thought he was going to lose the bet he had made with
Counts and Borischak about the top kick's dropping out.

"He's wobbling," said Hand. "Look at his shoulders sag.
The hike ain't over yet." And he let out a yell—the kind of
a yell Nathan Bedford Forrest's men let out when they at-
tacked the 15th Infantry's pocket at Shiloh. Nothing happened. "See?" said Hand. "He's too pooped even to bawl
me out. That shows how far gone he is. He'll never make
it."

I was beginning to wonder if I could make it myself. I
was glad there was no bet on me, glad that no wagerer was
watching my limp and grinning at my dragging feet. I en-
tertained thoughts of bayoneting General Castner some night
when he would happen along while I was on guard duty.
In a regimental daze, we left the railroad spur, heading
down Racecourse Road on the final stretch to the Compound.

"Steady, men, steady," said Lieutenant Curtis. "We've almost got it made. We'll be known as Flying E after this."

But just a block and a half before we reached the Compound
gate, our first sergeant fell down on the pavement and
couldn't get up again. He was out cold.

"Man, man," said Digby Hand, "them beers is gonna taste
good."

Lieutenant Curtis was desperate. "He's got to make it!
Counts, you and Borischak get him to his feet. Hand, you
take his pack. I'll help. Get him on his feet."

Hand jerked the pack from the prostrate sergeant. Counts,
Borischak, and Lieutenant Curtis hoisted him up from the
street. He came to and protested foggily and profanely that
he couldn't walk, but it did him no good. "You're in for the
duration, Top," said Counts. "Turn loose, Lieutenant. Me
and Borischak got him. We'll get him home."

Thus we of E Company finished the long march in a sort of mob formation, straggling a city block behind the rest of the regiment, our first sergeant dragged along by the two men he had the least faith in, the rest of us and our lieutenant shambling along as best we could. General Castner and his aides stood by the Compound gate as we tottered in. By that time, he had seen many men being helped along by their comrades, and now there was weariness aplenty in his own face as he looked us over. "They're tired," he remarked to his aides, "but they've still got lots of miles left in them."

At our barracks, we fell out for the last time that day, the duty sergeant who had taken over for the top kick giving the command. "Get the first sergeant to his bunk," said Curtis. After that had been done, he said to Counts and Borischak, "Thanks, boys, I knew I could depend on you."

Later, while we were at supper—those of us who had the stamina to tackle supper—Lieutenant Curtis came into the mess hall and told us what we had done. We had marched thirty-six and a half miles in about thirteen hours and broken the United States Army's peacetime infantry hiking record. The regiment had lost a hundred and twenty men out of the original nine hundred that had started. E Company was the only outfit to get back to the Compound at full strength. He, Curtis, was proud of us.

Hand, Counts, and Borischak argued over who had won the beer bet. Hand had wagered that the first sergeant would fall out—which he had. Counts and Borischak had wagered that he would finish the march—which he had.

"Well," said Borischak, "let's go get the beer and argue it out there. I know damn well me and Counts won."

I accompanied them as moderator. We went to the Café Genève. But we didn't walk. We took jinrikishas.

Brigadier General Joseph Compton Castner was born in 1869 and graduated from Rutgers in 1891. That same year he entered military service as a second lieutenant in the Fourth Infantry Regiment. He graduated from the Infantry and Cavalry School in 1895. Having gone up through the regular grades, he was promoted to brigadier general in 1921. He retired from the army in 1933 and died in 1938. At the time of the hike, he was nearly sixty years old. The question is: how could a man of his age walk the derrières off 899 men all younger than he was?

Well, hiking was his hobby. The story goes that as a young man around the turn of the century he had hiked from Alaska to Seattle, and, conceivably, was the only white man ever to have done so. The story further goes that he had started out with two Indian guides, but ended up with neither. One soon had become tired and had quit the party. A robust rumor circulated among the awe-struck infantry was that Castner had eaten the other when he had run short of food somewhere in the vicinity of the Great Slave Lake. Anyhow, in Tientsin on Sunday mornings the officers and ladies of the regiment customarily would take a genteel horseback ride at the Race Course. Castner would be there, too, but he wouldn't be riding. He would be hiking, pacing, pacing, pacing that bulk of his around the track, toning his leg muscles and timing himself.

It was a religion with him that infantrymen should march and know how to march. That was why he instituted the series of hikes which led up to the blockbuster. It had been his original intention to move his command—every man of it, if possible—on foot for one hundred miles in three days. But his command neither shared his marching ability nor his enthusiasm. After the first day's hiking was over, the Post Hospital was so crammed with crippled men that beds had to be set up in the Recreation Hall to care for the overflow. Nevertheless, General Castner was prepared to move out again the next morning with those who could walk, and he had had orders cut to that effect. But the orders were never issued. The Inspector General from the Philippines was on hand, and when he saw the shape the regiment was in and heard of the general's intent to put it on the move again, he told Castner flatly not to do it, and further told him he would cable Washington, if necessary, to prevent him. Castner bowed angrily to the edict and further hiking was called off for the nonce.

Even after thirty-two years, the memory of that hike still burns in the minds of the men who made it, as letters to me from retired "Can Do" men will testify. I ask myself now if I could have completed the projected one hundred miles. All I can say is that I might have been able to do so. But as to having been in any shape for fighting at the end of them—hell, no! How Stonewall Jackson and other Civil War chieftains ever got any fighting out of their men after the terrific forced marches they put them through will be forever beyond my comprehension.

Because of the hike and because the Inspector General happened to be on the spot to witness its results, the U. S. Army resurveyed the whole business of extended marches, and modifying orders were issued. Individual hikers easily can do one hundred miles in three days. They can set their own pace. General Castner, on our hike, was in a sense an individual marcher. He set his own pace. But the 899 men who trailed after him had to set their paces to match his, and that's what knocked so many of them out.

THE ORDERLY

6

There is still in existence a booklet entitled *Customs of the Fifteenth U. S. Infantry*. It was printed in Tientsin, by the Peiyang Press, *circa* 1930, under the aegis of Colonel James D. Taylor, then commanding officer of the regiment. I assume the adjutant compiled it under Colonel Taylor's direction. For some reason, it reminds one faintly of the *Spiritual Exercises* of Ignatius of Loyola. It is stark, dogmatic, hard in places to understand at this late date, and has no nonsense about it. It was passed out to the new officers when they reached the regiment, and they were ordered—not asked—to read it and digest it. The military historian, Edward Sprague Jones, in his preface to a facsimile of the booklet brought out by C. E. Dornbusch, military bibliographer, says: "[It] is a handbook of usage. It is neither recollection nor reconstruction, and is the only example of its kind about which we know."

Customs, says Mr. Jones, "clearly enunciates the individual's social obligation to the Regiment, and reciprocally, the Regiment's responsibility toward the individual with due regard to status." *Customs* even laid down what the regiment was to do in cases of births, marriages, and deaths among its members. The following chapter headings are indicative:

> Birth of a child of an officer.
> Birth of a child of an enlisted man.
>
> Death of an officer.
> Death of an enlisted man.

On the subject of orderlies, *Customs* had this to say: "*Commanding Officer's Orderly*. When a soldier has been selected as Commanding Officer's Orderly, he is granted by his company commander a twenty-four-hour pass, for the next day following his relief from guard. This Orderly Pass is honored at the post recreation hall as a free pass to the next moving picture show."

Customs didn't go into the business of how an orderly was chosen; it assumed, rightly so, that everyone knew how this daily honor was bestowed. Every day at noon, year in and year out, the guard was changed in the most solemn ceremony of the day. Sometimes the guard mount would be formal with music by the regimental band and a review by the commanding officer. Other times it would be informal, merely a transfer of duty by the old Officer of the Day to the new Officer of the Day. But, formal or no, at each guard mount a new orderly was chosen.

He was selected by the new Officer of the Day for his appearance, his military bearing, and the degree of polish evident in his buttons, his shoes, his cap visor, belt buckle, collar ornaments, rifle sling and rifle stock, bayonet, and ammunition pouch. Sometimes competition was so keen that the final selection was based on the degree of cleanliness of the competitors' fingernails. When one decided to buck for orderly in the 15th, one set for oneself something like a four-hour chore of preparation. "Sir, with the company commander's permission, I would like to buck for orderly today." "Very well. Fall out and return to the barracks and get at it."

There were six posts to be guarded in the Compound, and that meant three men for each post. Divided into three reliefs, each relief under a corporal, they would serve around the clock, two hours on post, four hours off. If you fouled up in any way while on sentry duty, the sergeant of the guard would "pull your belt"—literally jerk from you the web belt on which hung your bayonet and your ammunition pouch and was your badge of guard duty, and would march you to the guardhouse under arrest where you would await whatever punishment the officers chose to deal out. Interior guard was serious business. We all hated it, but every nine days we had to do it.

Selection of the orderly, of course, left one man shy in the detail, because the orderly reported at once to the commanding officer for duty. His vacancy had to be filled by the next man up on the duty roster. Hence, everybody had to stick around for guard mount, for nobody knew who would be picked for orderly or who would have to take his place on guard.

The orderly himself just sat on a chair outside the commanding officer's office, sometimes being sent on an errand but not very often. He did have to stand up and salute, however, whenever an officer came along the hall—which was frequent—so he had no chance to drop off into a nap. Being selected for orderly was an honor I was never able to achieve during my three years with the 15th. I bucked for it once or twice without even getting a look-in, but after that I was content with just getting by.

John Walsh, however, was chosen for orderly practically every time he went out for it. He was a big potbellied man with pop eyes and a bald spot, but, when he drew in his gut and squared his shoulders and slapped his rifle stock with his big hamlike hands, no one could compete with him for snap and effective appearance. He had some trick of converting himself from a fat, drunken slob into an impressively military-looking figure, and when the Officer of the Day finished inspecting the new guard and stood back to look the men over and pick the orderly, his eyes always came to rest on John Walsh.

I was a very new China hand when I first heard John Walsh lay down his rules about drinking. These were personal statutes he had formulated during his twenty years in the armed services, years which included cruises in the navy where he worked up to petty officer, and hitches in the infantry and the air corps, in which latter branch—lighter than air (dirigibles)—he had worked up to staff sergeant. He had never been able to rise higher than first-class private in the infantry, but it was the branch he loved best, and he always returned to it, particularly the 15th, when other forms of service palled on him. He was on his third return to China when I knew him.

His ideas about drinking were serious, for it was a way of life with him. He had just won ten or fifteen dollars in a poker game and was sitting on his bunk, shining his tunic buttons with Soldier's Friend. The squad coolie was off somewhere, and John was too much in a hurry to wait for him to come back and do the polishing. I said to him, "Are you bucking for orderly again, John? I thought you weren't due on guard for a couple of days yet."

"No, I ain't bucking for orderly, son," he said. "I'm just fixing to go out and slop up a few beers."

"But why all the shine then?"

Walsh carefully put his tunic on his bunk and picked up his shoes and began to go over them with a rag. "When a man comes off a drunk," he said, "he is generally the most despicable-looking animal in all creation. He'll be needing a shave, his uniform likely will be torn, and, torn or no, you can bet it'll be plenty rumpled. He'll be dirty, stinking dirty. The shine'll be gone from his shoes and his belt, and, if he still has his garrison cap, it'll be half tore apart. That's why when I go out to have a few beers I always police up like I was bucking for orderly. I never know, son, into what paths them few beers is gonna lead me, but I always see to it that old John Walsh is in proper uniform when he gets led. If you start out looking neat and clean, chances are you won't be quite so disreputable-looking when you get back."

"Where you going this time?"

"Guess I'll go and see Dutch Mamie. First time I went to her place was back in 1914. It was my first hitch here in Tientsin. The Germans was still here then, and we still wore the blues. Mamie was a young girl then, and I got into trouble on account of drinking too much beer. Three German privates was in her place, and they came at me with their belts. Well, nobody comes after John Walsh with a belt in his hand, German or no German. The chairs Mamie had in her bar in those days were good, heavy chairs, and the legs of 'em made good clubs. So it was old John Walsh with a chair in his hands and his back against the wall facing three German privates who was swinging their belts at him, leather belts with heavy brass buckles on the end. Oh, it wasn't a fair fight. There should have been at least four more German privates there to make it fair. After it was over, Mamie told me to not never come into her place again. Well, she was a German girl, and she had to stick up for her kind—even though they was laying on the floor with their heads busted open. They tried to court-martial me about it. Yessir, they tried to court-martial poor old John Walsh. There was a hearing, and a German oberlieutenant come to it. He wanted to charge that a whole gang of Yanks had teamed up on his men and laid them out. So we got Dutch Mamie in, and she and the oberlieutenant went at it in kraut, and the oberlieutenant got her good and mad right off the start, so she told the truth. When the oberlieutenant was finally convinced that it hadn't been a whole gang of Yanks, but just poor old John Walsh, why, he clicked his heels and walked away. It would of looked kind of funny, you know, to court-martial John Walsh for beating up three of the Kaiser's men. I got company punishment, though: three days' restriction to barracks. And they put Dutch Mamie's place out of bounds, and she like to starve till they opened it up again. Yes, I like to go to Dutch Mamie's and chew the rag about the old times. The Germans pulled out of Tientsin in 1914 and went to Tsingtao, and the Japs surrounded them there, and they had a fight. The Jap infantry charged, and the German machine gunners mowed 'em down. Nobody remembers much about it any more. But when it was over—the Battle of Tsingtao—Jap fighting against German on Chinese soil, they claim there was six dead Japs for every dead German. Anyhow, the Japs won that one, I think. Mamie should know all about it. I'll ask her when I'm in her place this afternoon."

"Will you be back for supper?" I asked.

"No, son, not for supper or breakfast or dinner or even supper the next day. I've been tightening up here lately, and I need to untighten. I'll be back in two–three days, though, and then I'll get a good rest in the guardhouse. The guardhouse here is fine; it's never crowded; you can take a shower every day; and the chow's fine. There ain't nothing to do but lay around on your bunk and chew the rag with your old friends. It's quiet there. I'll just plead guilty and throw myself on the mercy of the judge advocate and settle for fifteen days. No bother or anything. I figure I'll need that fifteen-day rest when I get back."

He carefully wrapped his puttees around his legs, put on a dickey, and adjusted his tie. Then he slipped on his tunic and gleaming leather belt.

"Let's see," he said, "by the time I get back it'll be K Company's turn to feed the prisoners. Howard Dobbs is mess sergeant. Known him off and on for fifteen years. I'll probably see him when I'm at Dutch Mamie's. I won't want much the first day I'm back, but the next day I'd like some good soup and some chicken. Yep. And the next day veal cutlets or maybe some frog legs. Then some roast pork. I'll draw up a menu for Howard Dobbs when I see him at Dutch Mamie's. He appreciates them things. We soldiered together in the navy on the old tanker *Pecos*. He wasn't a mess sergeant then—just a cosmoline slinger."

John Walsh cocked his Pershing cap slightly and gave himself a final critical inspection in the full-length mirror. "Reckon I'll pass muster," he said. And he tucked his swagger stick under his arm and went out the door. I looked out the window and watched him stride across the parade ground. He passed the commanding officer and gave him a snappy salute.

The Military Police brought him back four days later. He was in awful shape and came unprotestingly. He got his fifteen days in the guardhouse, just as he had planned. Mess Sergeant Howard Dobbs of K Company, faithful to the old trust, followed John's menu to the letter. During his stay in the guardhouse, Walsh missed two turns at guard duty. Thus, when he was released, his name was at the top of the duty roster.

I saw him sitting on his bunk, shining his buttons with Soldier's Friend.

"Good Lord," I said, "you're not going on another drunk, are you?"

"No, son," he said. "I'm bucking for orderly. It's time to get back to soldiering again." He bawled out the squad coolie, Short-timer, for not having his shoes shined the way he liked them. He examined his Springfield critically and applied more linseed oil to its stock. He borrowed my bayonet because it seemed a tiny bit more shiny than his. He drew in his gut and fastened his web belt tightly. He inspected himself in the full-length mirror and made a few adjustments here and there. Then he went out and joined the men lining up for the new guard. Because of his height, he stood at the head of the detail in the front rank. A lieutenant, new to the regiment, was Officer of the Day. After the usual inspection, he drew back a little to pick the orderly. He fidgeted around nervously, then inspected everyone's rifle again. Finally, he drew John Walsh and another

man forward three paces and put them through rifle drill. The other man looked as neat or neater than John, but the rifle drill was his downfall. Even from the distance of our barracks window, I could hear John Walsh slap his Springfield's stock with his big hamlike hands.

The new lieutenant went up to Walsh and tapped him and said, "Report to the commanding officer as orderly."

CIVILIAN CLOTHES

7

One winter—apparently when he couldn't think of anything else to do—the regimental commander ordered a language census taken in the 15th Infantry. Forms were made up and mimeographed and sent around to the companies; each enlisted man had to fill one out, telling which languages he spoke, and how fluently. It was easy for us Midwesterners; we put down English, and that was that. Karl Grahlberg, our senior duty sergeant, had a little more trouble. "Vell, English—yess, I poot dot down. Sherman? Yess, vot am I tinking? Natural, I shpeak Sherman. I poot dot down. French? Vell . . . vell, um, I undershtand it pretty goot, but der shpeaking iss somedimes *trés difficile*. Vell, I poot it down. Now vot? Czech. Sure, I shpeak Czech, only I don'dt wride it or read it none. I poot it down. Hoongarian? Nobody vot vasn't porn in dot damn country can shpeak Hoongarian. I don'dt poot dot down. Acgh, Gott! I forget Shinese! Bot I don'dt read dot; I shust talk it. Vell, I poot it down. Polish I know, too, but not so goot. Shid! I don'dt tink I poot Polish down."

It turned out, after the census was tabulated, that the members of E Company spoke eighteen different languages. G Company, the Foreign Legion, as we called it, spoke thirty-five and led the regiment linguistically. American-born men were in the minority in G Company. Nobody knew why; it just seemed to happen that over the years as replacements arrived and were sorted out, G Company got more Poles, Italians, Austrians, Russians, Lithuanians, Bulgars, Mexicans, French, Spaniards, Belgians, Australians, Montenegrans, and Icelanders than did any of the other outfits. Calling their roll would have posed a problem to most first sergeants, but not to G Company's. His name was Wrhviac, and, though he spoke only nine languages, he could pronounce anything, even if it was written in Sanskrit. We used to eavesdrop on G Company sometimes when Wrhviac was calling the roll. It was a great performance, and a pleasure to hear.

E Company, however, was unique in one of its members. This was Fat Feng, and none of the other companies could boast of anything like him, because he was Chinese. He had been born in San Francisco of third-generation parents and, legally, was as American as anyone else, but was still pure-blooded Chinese and not a whit ashamed of it. On his language form, he put down English and Chinese. This was true enough, but the Chinese he spoke was Cantonese, and the Chinese spoken in Tientsin was Mandarin, tongues as different as Italian is from Latin. The company coolies accepted Fat Feng as being as American as the rest of us and put up no protest at waiting on him. In fact, many of them addressed him as "Hsien Hsung," which means "honored sir" or "heaven born," according to whoever happens to be translating it for you. The coolies couldn't understand his Cantonese as well as they could his English, so he spoke to them mostly in the latter tongue. However, Fat Feng had a sharp ear, and it wasn't long until he became able to modify the nine tones of his Cantonese to the four tones of Mandarin; he could already read and write Chinese, the characters being the same everywhere, and he mastered Mandarin in rather short order. Fat Feng was a good soldier, and everybody liked him. Dressed in the army uniform, he was hard to tell from any other American serviceman.

His particular pal was Gus Krites. They had enlisted together in San Francisco where Krites had found himself on the rocks. They met in a restaurant in Chinatown. Fat Feng was unhappy about some family affair; Gus was at loose ends; they joined the army and left Chinatown for China.

On his language census sheet, Gus Krites put down English, Russian, German, Latvian, Polish, and French. In his home town of Riga, Latvian had been the family language, Russian the political language, German the commercial language, French the salon language, English the international language, and Polish the pig language. I asked him once what he meant by pig language. "Like farmer talk," he said.

In Riga, Krites had gone to school and later entered military service, for Latvia was free then and military service was compulsory. His name in those days had been Gustav Kreitskalt. When the First World War broke out, Krites's Latvian regiment became part of the National Unit which fought with distinction for Russia in 1915. After the war ended and the Bolshevik terror began, Krites and some of his relatives decided to pack up and leave. They came to America. Krites tried civil life for a while in Pennsylvania, but was unhappy in it, and went to sea. He was temporarily on the beach in San Francisco when he met Fat Feng and they signed up for the 15th Infantry. He was in his thirties when I knew him.

There was a large White Russian colony in Tientsin in those days, its members being refugees from the same Bolshevik revolution that had made Krites an expatriate. Except for the fur dealers, who were comparatively well off, they were a miserable lot for they had to compete with the Chinese for a livelihood, and the living conditions of many of them were no better than those of the coolies. Stateless people, they inhabited in near-ghetto fashion a walled warren called the Blue Compound about a mile from the American barracks. Many of them, by means of their women, who were not averse to prostitution, lived off what they could glean from the American soldiers (when the marines landed, they really ate high on the hog). Others brewed and sold vodka, or had little shops where they bartered and traded or cobbled. The Chinese tolerated their presence.

Fat Feng and Gus Krites, on their forays around Tientsin, soon discovered the White Russians, and, as the well-educated Fat Feng put it, began to do "social research" among them. Krites and the Russians had a lot in common—the Bolshevik blood bath for one thing—and Fat Feng went along as an interested spectator.

One day, a week or two after the language census, the regimental commander decreed that the enlisted men of the 15th could wear civilian clothing when not on duty, if the clothing was neat and presentable. This ruling had already been put in effect in army posts in the States, but it was with some reluctance that it was applied in North China. Even so, hardly any of us took advantage of it. It was different in the States where a man in uniform was looked on as a sort of a bum. In China the uniform was a mark of distinction. Few of us had brought civilian clothing along when we had embarked, and that which was for sale in the Tientsin shops was of a distinctly European cut and outrageously expensive. Our company tailor announced he could make civilian clothes, and several of the younger non-coms placed orders with him. But the clothes he turned out—modeled on pictures he found in American magazines—looked so weird that the purchasers of them wore them only once or twice and then tried to sell them at a discount to someone else.

After the order was issued, Fat Feng and Gus Krites put their heads together one afternoon and announced they were "going shopping." When they returned, they said, they would be in civilian clothes. "We won't even notice the rest of you punks. We won't even speak to you."

They headed for the Blue Compound, and they came back just before chow call. Fat Feng was dressed as a mandarin—black skullcap with white button, black gown, black brocaded jacket and white-soled slippers, and wonderful black fur cape. Gus Krites was dressed as a White Russian—gray, curly astrakhan cap, fancily embroidered muzhik shirt, floppy green pants tucked into high Cossack boots. The silly thing about it was that if you had seen them on the streets of Tientsin, you would have thought them to be exactly what they appeared—a well-to-do young Chinese and his relatively less well-to-do Russian *compadre*. In fact, that's what the company commander thought when he came back to his office and caught a glance of them in the dayroom. He summoned the first sergeant, who had not yet seen them, and said, "Now see here, Sergeant, we've got to draw the line somewhere. I suppose that Chink and that Russian are friends of some of the men, and, of course, we *want* our men to be friends with the civilians. But I don't know whether they ought to bring them into the barracks. I'm sure there's a rule or something against it. If there isn't, there ought to be. Now it's all right to bring in other soldiers from the other commands—we encourage *that* because one of our missions here is to establish good will. But I'm going to put my foot down about bringing in Russian and Chinese civilians. Like I say, we've got to draw the line; there's got to be a line somewhere, Sergeant, and I think we've reached it. Now you get rid of those chaps. Don't be tough about it, because I don't want to hurt their feelings; but get rid of them. It's almost supper, and they probably want to eat at the men's mess, but we just can't have it. Good God, once you open the door to that sort of thing, there'd be no end to it. So get rid of them now. I came back here to pick up the mess fund report. Where did you put it?"

The first sergeant, still unaware of what was going on and only befuddled by the captain's lecture, said grimly, "I'll get rid of somebody, sir," and he strode into the day-room, where Krites and Fat Feng were shooting pool and screaming and cursing at each other in Pidgin-Russian gib-berish, while the rest of us sat around and watched.

"You're going to have to break this up," said the sergeant to us onlookers. "I don't know who brought these guys in, or who told 'em it was all right to shoot pool in our dayroom; but the company commander has seen 'em, and he's burned up. So get 'em out of here and tell 'em not to come back. I'll say this: Whoever brought 'em in in the first place ought to be kicked good and hard in a certain spot, and maybe he will be."

Krites and Fat Feng still had their backs to him. "Melican non-com talkee-talk velly toughski," said Fat Feng. "Dom-brofski toughski," agreed Krites. "Gosponich radel-spinach rottski. I'll play the eight ball in the corner pocket."

The first sergeant grabbed them by the shoulders and

jerked them around. "Out!" he cried. "Both of you! When I find the guy that brought you in, I'll . . . " Then he recognized them, and we onlookers thought he was going to have a heart attack.

The captain heard the uproar and came into the dayroom. "Sergeant," he said, "I wanted this done a little more quietly. And why did no one call out 'Attention!' when I came into this dayroom? There's too much slackness around here, Sergeant. Not enough military discipline. Get rid of these men like I told you, and come into the office. I want to talk to you."

The first sergeant said, "Captain, with your permission, I place these guys under arrest; I'll prefer charges against them immediately."

"Oh, we can't arrest them, Sergeant. We've no jurisdiction. Besides, they've committed no offense. Just get them out of the barracks—out of the Compound. That's all that's necessary."

"But Godalmighty, sir! It's Gus Krites and Fat Feng! Can't you see, sir?"

The captain took another look. "Well!" he said. "Well! Yes! Now what in the hell is the meaning of this? What in the devil is this all about?"

Fat Feng and Krites stood mute.

"Speak up!" snarled the sergeant. "You heard the company commander, didn't you?"

"Well . . . uh," said Krites, "it was just a kind of joke, sir. The order said civilian clothes was okay. Me and Fat Feng . . ."

"That's enough!" said the captain. "You and Fat Feng thought you'd make fools out of someone. Well, you have. I hope you're satisfied. Sergeant, put these men under arrest. Restrict them to quarters. They are out of proper uniform."

The sizzling company commander sought to prefer charges against Krites and Fat Feng under the 96th Article of War which says, in effect, that if no specific offense is listed under which a man may be court-martialed, he can be tried "for any other reason" which the officers may dream up. But Krites and Fat Feng were never brought to trial. The judge advocate pointed out that they *had been* in civilian clothes, clothes such as were commonly worn in the city in which they were quartered; and, well, why not just let the thing end with company punishment where no written record was involved? There was no point in looking silly about the thing, particularly if it should come up for review. Our company commander, having had a chance to cool off, agreed.

In fact, the captain, who was a good guy as well as a good company commander, let them off with an official bawling out and imposed no company punishment at all. An official bawling out, more formally known as a reprimand, meant that they had to appear before him in his office in full uniform, stand at attention, and receive their dressings down while the lieutenant and the first sergeant listened in.

Company punishment would have meant restriction to barracks for twenty days, say, with some petty, menial jobs in the supply room thrown in. In the 15th Infantry in those days, it was rather hard to think up anything adequate in the way of company punishment. Assessing extra kitchen police duty was impossible; there wasn't any kitchen police duty in the first place. The Chinese mess coolies did it, and got paid for it. There weren't any fatigue details to which to sentence the culprits, such as unloading Quartermaster supplies or sweeping up the parade ground, because the Compound coolies did all that and got paid for it. No company commander would force his men to work alongside the coolies, for, if he did so, he would lose face; in the eyes of the coolies he would be no better than the men he had so degraded. So company punishment meant sending the offenders down to the supply room with instructions to tell the supply sergeant to put them to work. Usually, the last thing a supply sergeant wanted was to have to boss a couple of malfeasants around all day. Ours would always say, "Get behind that stack of foot lockers and keep to hell out of sight. There's some old magazines you can look at. I ain't going to have you messing up my stuff out here."

Fat Feng always relished the reprimand he and Gus Krites received after the affair in the dayroom. He committed it to memory and would deliver it, on request, over a bottle of beer. It went like this:

(Enter Pvts. Fat Feng and Gus Krites, garrison caps under left arms, tunics and breeches pressed, buttons, collar ornaments shining, belts, shoes gleaming; both men neatly shaved and with fresh haircuts. Seated: the company commander and the first lieutenant. Standing: the first sergeant. All faces very grave.)

Fat Feng (as he and Krites come to a halt before the

captain's desk, salute and click their heels): Sir, Privates Fat
Feng and Gus Krites report to the company commander for
an official reprimand, as directed by the first sergeant.

The company commander: Uh, yes—yes, of course. Stand
at ease. No! Stay at attention. Now, by God, you men
ought to be ashamed of yourselves, making a fool out of
that civilian dress order. I'm damned surprised at you, Krites,
and I'm surprised at you, too, Fat Feng. It's this thing of
always trying to make a fool out of some simple little ac-
commodation like the civilian clothes thing—which was
done for your benefit—that always infuriates the regimental
commander. And I can't say I blame him a single damned bit.
Now, both of you men are good soldiers, but when you do
a thing like that you make me ashamed that I'm your company commander. It makes me sick and ashamed. It reminds
me of the story of the Ordnance general who invented a
target-scoring device. He worked ten years at it, and per-
fected it. They tried it out at Monterey. It was to be a time-
saver and to eliminate all possibility of error in scoring
targets on the rifle range. Well, they had the thing set up,
and a lot of high officers were there to see how it worked
on its first test. They had a corporal—specially trained—
to operate it. The target shooting began, and the device
worked perfectly. And then some stupid private did something to it—nobody ever figured out what—and all the
crazy thing would do after that was score bull's-eyes, no
matter where the actual bullet might hit. The general who
invented it was sick. A colonel said, 'It took a brilliant officer
ten years of his life to perfect that thing, but it took an
enlisted man only five minutes to ruin it.' And that's the
way with this civilian clothes order. It took the regimental
commander a whole year of correspondence to get it applied
here, and you two damned near spoiled it in five minutes.
It would have been spoiled for keeps if the colonel had
heard about it. Like I say, I'm ashamed to be your company

commander, and I hope nothing like this ever happens again. If it does, it's going to mean trouble—real trouble. Are there any questions? Lieutenant, do you and the first sergeant feel like adding anything to my remarks? Very well then: Dismissed.

Gus Krites was the only man I ever knew to get married in the 15th Infantry. To do so, he had first to get the company commander's permission and then the chaplain's. The girl was a White Russian, dark, pretty, and hairy, named —or at least called—Polya. She and Krites had a lot in common; members of both their families had been killed in the Bolshevik affair of 1917, back in Russia. They met in the Blue Compound and fell in love over several bottles of vodka. A matter of religion stood between them: she was Russian Orthodox, Krites was Lutheran. The lovesick Gus surmounted this by abandoning grand old Martin's teachings and taking instructions from the lips of the Patriarch of Tientsin, an expatriate prelate from the Volga who served Tientsin's White Russian colony. In fact, it was the patriarch who pleaded Krites's cause with the 15th Infantry's chaplain, a High Church Episcopalian. He pleaded so successfully that the chaplain took it up with the company commander, muttering something to the effect that it was better to marry than to burn. "Yes, Chaplain," said the frank company commander, "but, damn it all, I just can't see an American boy marrying one of those pigs."

Krites, the chaplain pointed out, was hardly a boy any more, being well into his thirties, and the American label was . . . well . . . rather honorary at best. "But what in hell are they going to live on?" demanded the company commander. "All Krites has is his private's pay."

Krites, the chaplain said, had a position promised him with a Russian (White) fur jobber; Krites intended to buy out of the army when he had enough time in. But he didn't want to wait that long to be married.

"You're very persuasive, Chaplain," said the company commander.

"It's the patriarch who's persuasive," said the chaplain. "I think he sees some political advantage accruing to him if one of his flock marries an American boy."

"American, my foot," said the company commander. "Krites is a Lithuanian or something."

"Latvian," corrected the chaplain. "Anyhow, he wears the American Army uniform and is entitled to an American passport when he gets his discharge."

"So he does. So he does. Well, let 'em get married then. I suppose it will work out all right. Must I attend the ceremony and bestow my blessing?"

"It would be nice of you to attend. The patriarch will take care of the necessary blessings."

So Gus Krites and Polya were married at a Nuptial Mass in the Russian Orthodox Church of Tientsin, a tiny, domed, mosquelike thing of jeweled Byzantine beauty. Fat Feng and I attended, as well as many other members of the company, including the captain. There was a feast afterward, during which I so bravely tackled the vodka that it was not long until I could not tell a kasatska from a polmenyi. Poor though those White Russians might have been, when they celebrated a wedding they never spared the troikas.

Krites moved into the Blue Compound with his bride and, in due time, secured his discharge from the army by means of purchase. That meant he had to pay back his clothing allowance and some other things he had received on enlistment. His fur jobbers gave him an advance to do so. He did so well in the fur business (Tientsin was then the fur capital of the world) that the jobbers made him a buyer, sending him out in the far places to round up pelts. He sent me a picture later, taken near Tsitsihar in Manchuria, of Polya and himself. They were mounted on Mongolian ponies. Dressed in furs, laughing and vigorous, they looked as if they might have been members of Genghis Khan's Golden Horde.

Fat Feng, too, bought out of the army. After he had been in for two years, his family troubles back in San Francisco settled themselves (apparently a hatchet man from Shanghai had something to do with the settling thereof), and his family wanted him back in Chinatown to manage their basket shop. He took a civilian ocean liner back to the States, traveling by train to Shanghai to catch it. Before he boarded the train, he said his last good-byes to the company. He had dressed himself as a mandarin—as he had been dressed that time in the dayroom when he and Gus Krites had aroused the wrath of the company commander and the first sergeant.

This time the captain wasn't angry. He grinned at Fat Feng and shook his hand, and told him he would look him up when he himself returned to San Francisco.

THE GATE

8 ❊

In Fort Benning, Georgia, just across the street from the Infantry School's main building and adjacent to the Officers' Club, there stands a memorial gate. A "gate" in name only, it is formed of two legs with a comparatively massive crosspiece sitting upon them; it looks something like an altar cut in half lengthwise. It stands about hat-high to the average soldier, and is made of white marble. Carven flowers adorn its legs. Inscriptions in both Chinese and English are chiseled into the crosspiece. A bronze plaque mounted in front of it says:

PRESENTED TO THE INFANTRY SCHOOL
by the
15th U S INFANTRY
(The "Can Do" Regiment)
ON ITS RETURN TO THE UNITED STATES
on March 24, 1938

AFTER OVER A QUARTER CENTURY OF
SERVICE IN CHINA

On the gate itself, the top inscription says: "A Remembrance of the Golden Deeds Done by Officers Men United States Forces in China."

Beneath that inscription, and on the right-hand side, a poem in Chinese characters is graven. On the left is the English translation thereof:

All the militarists struggled for a piece of ground,
Thus the wheel of fate was made to turn around.
At Shanhaikuan the battle furious was fought,
To Tientsin and Peking the danger was brought.
Soldiers defeated ran for their lives everywhere,
But fear of robberies the folks could not bear.
O innocent creatures peaceful rulers of the country,
Many a time 'mid the nightly alarm had to stay.
The sons of Uncle Sam so gallant in their deed,
Day and night to strict defense took the greatest heed.
And through their strenuous efforts and suffering
Peace among all was kept and maintained.
Honor to those to whom honor is due
For their good records were none too few.
Their golden fame spreads to east and west,
May each of them the Almighty bless.

This poem must have lost something in the translation. It just can't be that bad in its original Chinese. However, it's the thought, and not the metrical package, which counts.

This gate was presented originally to the 15th U. S. Infantry Regiment in April, 1925, while the regiment was in Tientsin. It commemorated the successful carrying out of one of the regiment's assignments in North China: to protect Tientsin from the incursions of leaderless, marauding Chinese troops. In order to keep such troops out of Tientsin, they first had to be kept out of the little villages which bordered Tientsin. The problem was particularly acute during the Chihli-Fengtien War of 1924–25. Because of the regiment's activities in those days, the grateful elders of some of the little villages in the American-guarded sector presented the gate to the regiment as an earnest of their appreciation.

As the poem on the monument which now stands at Fort Benning says, "All the militarists struggled for a piece of ground." When they succeeded in taking that piece of ground, i.e., city or town, it was customary for a "rape" to take place. This was the standard way in which the warlords rewarded their successful troops. Some of the rapes, by 1924, had become historic, viz, the Rape of Nanking, the Rape of Lanchow, the Massacre and Rape of Tsinanfu.

The word "rape" as used here is as explicit as can be found; it means exactly what it is intended to mean, and no further details are needed. Word of new rapes spread rapidly in those days, and the small villagers became nervous when the troops of the warlords approached too closely.

In 1924, civil war flamed across North China. The armies of Field Marshals Chang Tso-lin, Wu Pei-fu, and Feng Yu-hsiang were involved. The major area of battle was in Hopeh (then Chihli) Province, which contains the huge cities of Peking and Tientsin, the seaports of Shanhaikwan, Taku and Chingwangtao, and the great coal fields of Tongshan. To the north of Hopeh Province beyond the Great Wall lies Manchuria. Chang Tso-lin was warlord of Manchuria. To the west of Hopeh Province lies Shensi Province. Feng Yu-hsiang (also known as the Christian general) was warlord of Shensi. To the south of Hopeh Province lies Honan Province. Wu Pei-fu was warlord of Honan, and also called himself commander-in-chief of the army and navy of China. Far, far to the south, Chiang Kai-shek, who now rules over Formosa, was playing footsy with the Communists. He took no part in the civil war of 1924–25.

Wu Pei-fu, who called his policy the "Salvation of China," held Peking by virtue of his forces which occupied the city. To implement his Salvation policy, he had another policy called "Unity by Force," which, simply stated, meant war. After a high-level meeting with the Christian general, Feng, Wu decided to put the Unity policy into effect. This meant the conquest of Manchuria, where, behind the Great Wall, Chang Tso-lin lay like a tiger in its lair. Feng agreed to join Wu in carrying out the conquest. Wu ordered one of his armies to move into position at Shanhaikwan, the northern terminus of the Great Wall, to keep Chang bottled up. A second army was to jump the Wall west of Shanhaikwan and stir things up, while Christian General Feng's men moved up through Jehol Province and clamped a grip on northern Manchuria. Wu intended, through this three-pronged assault, to have done with Chang once and for all.

The armies began to move. The railways through Tientsin were jammed with troop trains, the Hai River with troop barges, the anchorage off Taku (Tientsin's seaport) with troop transports. All across North China, the troops of Warlord Wu Pei-fu were aswarm. In the Concessions of Tientsin, the foreign garrisons waited and watched. There was nothing else they could do. The Chinese troops in Tientsin were held under strict discipline by their officers, and there was no pillaging and no trouble. They stayed in Tientsin's "Native City" and kept out of the Concessions.

Everything went well for Wu Pei-fu until October 23, 1924. On that day, Wu himself was at Shanhaikwan, ready to give the signal for the all-out drive into Manchuria. But, on that day, came news about Feng Yu-hsiang. The Christian general had defected. Instead of advancing through Jehol Province into northern Manchuria, he had advanced into Peking, by then denuded of Wu's troops, and had taken over the great city. There he sat tight, and proclaimed himself boss of North China. Wu's second army refused to jump the

Great Wall west of Shanhaikwan until the situation was clarified. That left Wu alone at Shanhaikwan to face the entire Fengtien army of Chang Tso-lin, an army so-called because its headquarters were in Fengtien, Manchuria, the city more commonly known throughout the Occident as Mukden.

In a ripsnorting, hell-for-leather battle, the Fengtien army knocked the wadding out of Wu's forces (an enagement duly noted in the inscription on the 15th's memorial gate). Wu, by boat, train, donkey cart, and horseback, moved what army he had left back toward Peking to have it out with the Christian general. On the plains west of Tientsin, Feng Yu-hsiang's Shensi army crashed into poor Wu's oncoming tattered battalions, and administered one of those defeats which is known as "utter." Marshal Wu made it to the port of Taku with a few picked bodyguards and sailed away on his last remaining transport—into oblivion.

Now, out on the alluvial plain west of Tientsin, King Chaos reigned. Wu's remnants fled, as the saying goes, in all directions. Feng's Shensi army harried them from one side; Chang's Fengtien units harassed them from the other. They were like a scattered hatching of chickens with hawks darting at them from all angles. Sometimes, in the general melee, a Shensi detachment would meet a Fengtien force; each would slam into the other, and the losers would join Wu's fragments in fleeing over the plain.

The magnet which drew the shattered armies was Tientsin, rich, bursting with food and clothing, unpillaged, unraped. All across the plain, bands of leaderless, hungry, despairing men, hiding by day, skulking by night, began to converge on the great city.

This had been foreseen by the foreign army commands in Tientsin. The menace to the city was well understood. Accordingly, units of the international forces—American, British, French, Italian, and Japanese—were thrown into a loose cordon around the outskirts of Tientsin with orders to keep disorganized Chinese troops drifting in from the plain—Wu troops, Shensi troops, Fengtien troops, it made no difference—out of and away from Tientsin. This meant the literal establishment of token barricades at every means of ingress: road, canal, railway track, river, or dike. The 15th Infantry's sector was along the southern edges of the city. The main features of the terrain there were the Wei Ching Ho Canal, a dike paralleling the canal, and, beyond canal and dike, the Tientsin-Pukow Railway line. The commander of the 15th Infantry Regiment in those days was a lieutenant colonel named George Catlett Marshall.

Along an arc some seven miles in length, the 15th set up five outguard posts, each with a food station where rice and cabbage would be traded to the dispersed Chinese troops in return for whatever weapons they might be carrying. Once they were disarmed they would be allowed to proceed around the Concessions to a kind of a camp in the Native City. In between the outguard stations were Cossack posts, formed of a corporal and two privates who were to act as lookouts only. The main business was to be conducted at the outguards, but the main strength of the regiment was kept in reserve in the American Compound, where the troops were barracked, under combat pack, ready to move. If the outguards couldn't handle the situation with rice, this reserve would move out and handle it with bullets.

I had not yet got to China in those days, but, when I did arrive in 1927, the veterans of the outguards were still talking about their experiences and had no reluctance at all to reminisce at great length and with wealth of detail—over a bottle of nice, cool beer.

One who had played more or less of a key role was E Company's senior duty sergeant, the linguist Karl Grahlberg. As a much younger man, he had served in the Kaiser's Imperial Guard, and in the First World War he had won an

Iron Cross. However, as did many of his German companions-in-arms, he left the Fatherland after its defeat and migrated to the United States. Soldiering was all he knew, and he joined the U. S. Army. When he came to the 15th, he came in the grade of sergeant. Once, during field exercises at Nan-Ta-Ssu, where the 15th used to go for summer training, he captured two machine-gun nests with his platoon in a single morning. The referee, a gray, embittered colonel from the Philippines, made him do it again in the afternoon with the rest of the battalion watching, so that the men might see how it was done. The machine-gun nest commander, after his third surrender to Grahlberg, said complainingly to the referee, "By God, sir, he couldn't of done it if we had been using live ammunition." Karl heard him, and said, "No? Vell, py Gott, you ask dem Belchums vot vass at Namur."

The first three outguards were manned by E Company men, Karl commanding the first, Lieutenants Burrowes and Dabney commanding the second and third. Because of the lay of the land and the position of the roads, it was held doubtful whether Karl's outguard would see any "action" at all. His station was at a little walled village, some three miles from Tientsin, named Hai Niu Cheng. Translated, Hai Niu Cheng means Black Cow Village. It sat behind a dike. The dike bordered the Wei Ching Ho Canal. On the other side of the canal was a road. Beyond the road, a mile or so out on the plain, was the Tientsin-Pukow Railway line—out of operation during the current civil war. A camel-back bridge over canal and dike provided access from the plains to the Black Cow Village. This was what Sergeant Karl Grahlberg and his men were to guard.

Karl's detail consisted of a platoon of riflemen—three squads of eight men each, one of the men being a corporal and another an automatic rifleman—and a machine-gun crew of three privates and a corporal. Thus, his firepower consisted of twenty-one Springfield rifles, three Browning automatic rifles, one heavy Browning water-cooled machine gun, his own Colt .45 automatic pistol, and the four similar Colts of the machine gunners. His interpreter, Jughead, E Company's No. 2 boy, was unarmed.

For those days, that was rather potent armament for such an outguard. Karl's riflemen—experts and sharpshooters all —could pick a man off at six hundred yards on the flat, treeless plain that spread out from the dike. His automatic riflemen could impose a fire-hose effect at shorter ranges. His machine gun could enfilade a column, or could sweep the ranks of a line, or could reach out fifteen hundred yards in overhead, plunging fire. Dug in, he would have been a tough man to dislodge without employing artillery; and the stragglers on the plain had no artillery with them. As a matter of truth, however, Karl's force was as impotent as a rattlesnake which has had its fangs freshly pulled. In their cartridge belts, his riflemen carried blocks of wood. In the machine gun's belt was dummy ammunition. The magazines of the automatic rifles were empty, and so were the magazines of all the big Colt pistols—except Karl's own. His contained five rounds. The high command didn't want Karl to initiate a war of his own out there in the hinterland. If he was to carry out his mission, he would have to carry it out by bluff alone.

However, he was supplied with fat sacks of rice and a dozen baskets of cabbages and many blocks of tea. With these as weapons, he was to bribe the oncoming hordes to give up their firearms and take a forty-mile detour around Tientsin.

Karl marched his men at daylight to his outguard station proper, a mud and brick hong near the camel-back bridge which spanned the dike and canal near the Black Cow Village. A mule-drawn forager's wagon rumbled along behind, carrying his men's bedding and food and water casks, his sacks of rice, his baskets of cabbages, his bricks of tea, and his field stove. A little donkey pulled the machine gun in its cart.

The hong was commodious and could sleep about twenty men at a time on army cots and still allow room for a mess table. Strictly speaking, it wasn't a hong at all, because real hongs are mercantile warehouses providing a series of connecting rooms, and Karl's hong had only the one room. The Black Cow villagers used it as a storehouse for vegetables and grain, but it stood empty now, for the villagers, fearful that the soldiers of the plain might loot it, had emptied it of its stores and secreted them in the Black Cow Village itself.

Once he got there, Karl ordered his men to stack arms and unload the forager's wagon. Then he bethought himself of what he was there for, said, "Ach, Gott!" halted the unloading process, planted his machine gun on the dike, planted an automatic rifleman farther down the dike, told off a squad to dig foxholes in the dike, posted a sentinel on top of the camel-back bridge, and then went on with his housekeeping chores.

There was no place to stable the little donkey which had pulled the machine-gun cart. After the forager's wagon was unloaded, Karl had the donkey put into it and sent back to the stables at the American Compound. The beast heehawed mournfully as the soldiers picked it up bodily and thrust it through the letdown end gate into the big vehicle. Back at the stables, it sulked all the time because it was only happy when it was near its beloved water-cooled Browning. It liked to lick the grips of the weapon where the machine gunners' sweaty hands had deposited a film of salt.

Karl put a squad of men to work on the hong itself. The floor was swept out; the walls were swept down. Two kerosene lanterns were hung from a ceiling beam. Cots were set up with mattresses, sheets, blankets, and pillows. The portable stove was set up outside under a tent fly. Karl had brought along sacks of coal with which to stoke it, for there was little fuel to be found around the Black Cow Village.

The hong had a tile roof with a wavy ridge; and on the ridge, at strategic intervals, porcelain gargoyles were placed to keep the demons away. Many demons were known to lurk in the air above the Black Cow Village.

The camel-back bridge which arched over the dike and the canal was constructed of stone and wood, rather roughly made, but full of that inherent beauty the Chinese capture in every bridge they fashion. Private Digby Hand of Arkansas was the sentinel Sergeant Grahlberg had chosen to station there. Hand was an expert with both the Springfield rifle and the bayonet. After the hong had been cleaned out and furnished to suit him, Karl went up to the bridge to see how Digby was getting along. "I make a mighty good target up here, Karl," Hand pointed out. "I betcha if you was out on the plain, you could see me from three miles off." "Dot iss vot you iss here for," said Sergeant Grahlberg. "First dey shoot you, den ve shoot dem. Shust like dot." "These here wooden bullets of mine don't carry so far," said Hand. "How about my tradin' 'em in for a stack of rocks to throw?" "You got nobody to t'row at yet," said Karl. "Shust keep der eyes peeled und don'dt talk so motch."

While this was going on, the Black Cow Village had emptied itself of everything that could walk, limp, crawl, or be carried, and all had come to Karl's hong to watch and wonder and speculate over what was going on. In those days in North China, you couldn't do anything without attracting as an audience every Chinese seemingly within telegraphic distance, and this was no exception. Whenever one of Karl's men dropped a cigarette butt on the ground, there was a scramble for it which sometimes ended up in fisticuffs. The mayor of the Black Cow Village came forth and asked to talk with the American commander. Karl sum-

moned Jughead, the No. 2 boy, to interpret, but the mayor
waved him away. He could speak better English than Jughead could. Karl briefed the mayor on the situation and
told him the American Army would pay for the use of the
hong. The mayor smiled and said pay was unnecessary. The
Black Cow Village was honored by the Americans' presence.
The mayor also decided that the occasion was a gala one—
here were all these sturdy Mei Kuo (American) soldiers
guarding his village—and, after a few words more with
Karl Grahlberg, he returned to his village and ordered the
kites to be flown.

The Chinese are the greatest kite-makers and kite-fliers
on earth. Into the lazy, slightly dusty air above and around
Karl's hong, the kites went up—scores of them. Some were
box kites as big as piano crates. Some were dragon kites
made in three sections so that the heads and tails could waggle
—which they did—and gave a very eerie effect some forty
feet off the ground. Some were butterfly kites with spread-
ing, gossamer-like, beautifully tinted wings. Some were castles
which looked as if they wouldn't fly at all, but which went
shooting up to startling altitudes. Nearly all the kites had
whistles or chimes attached to them. In a matter of moments,
the air was full of color and motion, as if a rainbow had
been shattered there and the pieces of it hung in the sky.
And a soft, unearthly whistling, chiming music floated down,
as if the air were full of oriental cherubim. The mayor
brought Karl a gourd full of melon seeds, and other elders of
the village brought out little earthenware jugs of *tsa-ju*,
Chinese wine made from kaoliang roots and spiced and
fermented until it could eat the shellac off an oar. "*Nein,
nein,*" said Karl to the soldiers who accepted the *tsa-ju*,
"poot dot stuff avay. Dot's an order." The soldiers took the
little jugs into the hong where Karl couldn't see them,
and tried to pry the cork out of one of them with a bayonet. The little flagon broke into pieces, and the *tsa-ju*,

which has an odor as far-reaching and penetrating as that of civet musk, ran all over the floor. It even wafted itself to the nose of Digby Hand on lookout on the camelback bridge. "What the hell's going on down there?" he yelled, looking at the kites and the swarms of the Black Cow villagers, and sniffing the *tsa-ju*. "It looks like a chivaree in the Ozarks instead of an outguard. You better break it up, Karl; Wild Bill's liable to be along any minute on inspection."

Wild Bill was Captain William B. Tuttle who, in addition to his other duties, commanded the 15th Infantry's Mounted Patrol, an elite (or at least they considered themselves elite) group of ex-cavalrymen, who were provided with Manchurian ponies for steeds and whose duty it was to act as scouts for the regiment. It was Wild Bill's personal duty that day to make preliminary inspections of the outguards after they had been set up. Wild Bill, in those days, was probably the most popular officer in the regiment. He was athletically good-looking, a superb horseman, and had a genial, relaxed way about him that the men instinctively liked. He could be tough if he wanted to, but it was the kind of toughness which brings respect and doesn't inflict humiliation.

As foretold by Digby Hand, he soon came riding down the dike on Gobi Sun, the buckskin-colored Manchurian stallion which he had trained to be the best polo pony in North China. Booted, spurred, bepistoled, his campaign hat tightly held down by its chin strap, his field Sam Browne belt supporting canteen and first-aid kit, he jumped Gobi Sun off the dike and pulled up in front of the hong, where Sergeant Grahlberg saluted him. Wild Bill loosened his chin strap and pushed back his campaign hat, sniffed the *tsa-ju*, eyed the crowd and the kites, and said, "My God, Karl, are you celebrating a wedding, or what the hell?"

"Vell, sir," said Karl, "I don'dt like it none neider, but I shust can't help it. Dey shust come from efferyvhere und fly dem damn kites. Dey . . . dey iss happy, sir."

"Happy?" said Wild Bill. "Hell, they're in a state of ecstasy. But they won't be so happy if a couple of hundred hungry casuals descend on 'em and do like they did at Lanchow. You're here to prevent that, you know, Karl, and not to fly kites and guzzle *tsa-ju*."

"I don'dt fly no kite, sir, und I don'dt guzzle noddings," said Karl indignantly. "I shust do vot I can do, und dot's all. Here, sir, I show you."

And he pointed out to Captain Tuttle the disposition he had made of his forces: the machine-gun nest on the dike, the accompanying nests for the automatic riflemen, the foxholes for the men armed with Springfields. "If I had bullets, Captain Tuttle," he said, "I vould take on a whole damn Shinese regiment. I mean dot, sir!"

"I know you do, and I don't doubt in the world but what you could do it," said Wild Bill. "I don't like this wooden ammunition stuff any more than you do. But it's orders." He took a map from his musette bag. "Here, help me hold this damned thing. You're here. Burrowes is down there. Dabney's there, and so on. But it's right here that concerns you. There are at least four bands of irregulars—Wu's boys, we think—out on the plain in this direction. There may be two thousand; there may be only two hundred. Our 'intelligence' isn't certain. They are hid out now, but, if they march all night tonight, they could be here early tomorrow morning. We think they're headed for Taku where there may be a boat or two left. We thought they'd hit Burrowes' outguard first, and that's why we put him there. But it looks now like you'll be the welcoming committee. It doesn't make a hell of lot of difference; Burrowes doesn't have any ammunition, either.

"The point is, you mustn't let them cross the canal and the dike; you've got to keep them following the general line of the railway, and make them stay out of Hai Niu Cheng here. You'll bounce 'em down to Burrowes, and he'll bounce 'em down to Dabney, and Dabney'll bounce 'em to the British; and to hell with them after that. We'll have mounted patrols out to see that they stick to their detour. If they don't, we'll call up the battalion from the Compound, and the shooting may start. We'll see to it that *you'll* have some ammunition if that should happen. We're going to string a telephone line out to you tomorrow. We've already got a line out to Dabney. When, and if, those irregulars do get here, you are to tell them you will give them rice and cabbage if they will give up their arms. You have already been briefed on that. It's in your written orders. But—no guns, no rice. We figure they'll be hungry enough to trade. At least, our 'intelligence' says so. Any questions?"

"Vell, yes, sir. Dot rice, Captain Tuttle. Should I shust giff it to dem raw, or should I better cook it for dem first?"

"Oh . . . cook it first, I guess, and serve it with treacle."

"Ve don'dt got no treacle, sir."

"No? Well, leave off the treacle then."

"Vun more t'ing, sir. If dese Shinese got officers mit dem, do I salute dose officers, or turn out der guard for dem, or shust say 'sir' to dem, or vot der hell?"

"Well, as a matter of military courtesy, I'd say salute 'em, yes. But it's up to you. Nobody thought of *that* before, so there's no specific orders to cover it. But I'll tell you one thing, Karl: Colonel Marshall will be along sometime tomorrow morning to inspect, and you better turn out the guard for *him*. And you know how he inspects. You better hide the kites and the melon seeds before he gets here."

"Yes, sir."

"One other thing. You know how Colonel Marshall hates flies! If he finds a single fly in that hong of yours, it could mean your stripes, Karl."

"He von'dt find no flies, sir."

"Well, he better not." And Wild Bill Tuttle swung onto

Gobi Sun, jumped the stallion to the top of the dike, and rode off.

There began to be considerable traffic along the canal road, and on the canal itself. On the road were two-wheeled donkey carts, basket carriers, wheelbarrows, and the like. On the canal were narrow, flat-bottomed, shallow-draft barges being poled along by coolies or towed by coolies on the canal path. The waterway there was about ten feet wide. Traffic jams on it were continuous. Digby Hand, from his lookout post atop the camel-back bridge, surveyed the water-borne confusion with mounting interest, giving directions and yelling at the coolies as the occasion seemed to warrant. "Stabbard yer hellum! Gee yer coolie team! Reverse yer enjines! Yer clearly in the wrong there, skipper. Yield the right of way."

After he tired of that, he looked out on the plain, and his keen Arkansas eyes spotted a tightly knit group of strange-appearing vehicles. He took a second long look, then let out a yell to Sergeant Grahlberg. "Mortar platoon, Karl! Heading this way. They're on the double!"

Sergeant Grahlberg, who had been busy directing things at the field kitchen, chambered a cartridge in his service pistol, summoned a corporal with an empty Springfield, and mounted the bridge to see for himself. "Two barbers und a sveet-potato seller," he said after his inspection. "Vot a hell uf a goot lookout ve got."

The barbers pushed their equipment in two-wheeled barrows with themselves harnessed between the shafts. The sweet-potato seller pushed his on a mammoth one-wheeled barrow, the wheel being in the middle, brazier being at one end, potatoes at the other. "They looked a hell of a lot like a mortar outfit at first," said Digby Hand in self-defense. Karl Grahlberg sniffed.

Quite a crowd had been gathered at the foot of the camel-back bridge, and this was what had attracted the three small businessmen on the plain. Quickly, barbers and sweet-potato seller stabilized their barrows by letting the vehicles' legs down into the dirt, and set up shop with quiet efficiency. Candy vendors and bread vendors came along and joined them. Boatmen on the canal, travelers on the road stopped and made little purchases or little sales. The place took on the appearance of an open-air market. Everybody had a nice time except Karl Grahlberg. He was trying to tell them that there was a war on, but nobody would listen.

He called up his interpreter Jughead and tried to elicit from the ones who had been out on the plain whether they had seen any soldiers there. Some said yes, they had seen swarms of them, heavily armed, murderous devils, one and all. Others said they hadn't seen a single one. But one and all joined in asking the American sergeant if a great battle was to be fought here at the threshold of Hai Niu Cheng. If so, they intended to stay right on the spot so as not to miss any of the excitement.

"Vot a hell uf a mess," said Karl. "All ve need now iss for Colonel Marshall to come along."

But the colonel didn't show up, and the day dragged along, and Karl changed his outguard shifts every two hours, one squad of riflemen and a machine gunner on the dike at all times, the other two squads and the other machine gunners resting in the hong. At sundown, the crowd became convinced that nothing was going to happen and dispersed, even the Black Cow villagers retiring behind their village walls. Karl's sentinels, atop camel-back bridge and dike, had the black night to themselves. Twice during the night, at 11 P.M. and at 3 A.M., gunfire could be heard out on the plain. But that was all that happened.

At sunup, the crowd began to gather again in twos and threes. The barbers and the sweet-potato seller reappeared and set up business again. A coolie tow-team came down the canal bank, pulling a long barge piled high with kaoliang.

A few kites floated up over the Black Cow Village. Karl bestirred his men. "Dey eider come or dey don'dt come," he said, referring to the casuals on the plain. "But ve got to be ready for dem if dey do come. So now ve cook some rice." It turned out that while his men were adequately schooled in the cooking of bacon and eggs and the preparing of coffee, none of them knew how to cook rice. Everyone knew you boiled it, but none knew exactly how. "Vell, Jughead knows," said Karl. "Jughead iss a Shinaman, und all Shinamen can cook rice." And he called Jughead and ordered him to prepare a washtub full of boiled rice for the expected arrival of the hungry irregulars.

The portable field stove had been set up under a tent fly near the foot of the camel-back bridge on the Black Cow Village side of the dike. Jughead disdainfully put a kettle of water on it, waited for the water to boil, and threw in handfuls of rice. The rice fluffed up and ran over the sides of the kettle. Every fly in that part of North China came buzzing in to join the feast. "Goot Gott!" said Karl. "Look at all dem damn flies! If Colonel Marshall should come now—Gott!"

He ordered three of his men back to the hong to keep any straying flies away from there, or suffer for it with their lives. He looked doubtfully at the rice itself. The barbers and the sweet-potato seller were standing nearby. Karl asked them if they would like a sample. One barber hesitantly tried a taste, and spat it out. The sweet-potato seller then tried one, and likewise spat it out. "Vot's der matter?" demanded Karl. "Ain'dt it no goot?"

"They say I no cook it right," said Jughead indignantly.

"Hokay! Let dem cook it demselves den. You tell dem, Jughead, dot now dey got to cook." And Karl Grahlberg slapped his pistol holster.

Jughead translated the order. At once a loud argument

broke out between barbers and sweet-potato seller. "Now vot?" asked Karl.

"Is the pan," said Jughead. "Potato man say pan must be wide, wide. Barber say pan must be deep, deep. They come from different cities," he offered by way of explanation.

"To hell mit der pan!" exploded Karl. "Tell dot potato man to cook, und cook qvick, or I shoot hiss head off!"

Proud of being selected, the sweet-potato man began to cook rice; and the barbers stood by and criticized; and more kites floated up over the Black Cow Village. The mayor, dressed in his best black gown, came up and politely asked Sergeant Grahlberg why all the *fan* (rice) was being prepared. Some gala event, he assumed. Karl told him the real reason. The mayor's face took on a quizzical look. The Americans intended to feed the ravaging hordes of Wu and Feng and Chang? How odd. He took a sharp look at the sweet-potato man and at his rice-cooking technique. It was hardly the way a Black Cow villager would cook rice, he said. But he shrugged. It was probably good enough for soldiers.

Then, something peculiar happened. Digby Hand was to talk about it for years later. He is probably still talking about it, for he would be only in his early sixties now.

"One time when I was a kid back in Arkansas," he would say, "I was watching a bunch of jaybirds out in the grapevines. They was eating and fighting and pecking at each other, and having a big time in general. Then, all of a sudden, one of them went 'Chrrr! Chrrr! Chrrr!' real quick and real soft like. Pretty soon, they was all going 'Chrrr! Chrrr! Chrrr!' Then, in a flock, they all took off. I wondered what the hell had spooked them. In about five seconds I found out. It was a chicken hawk, and it came flying in low, just over the grapevines. But by then, all the jaybirds had gone.

"It was the same thing there by that damned camel-back bridge. There was all the Chinese standing around our field stove and the tent fly, laughing, talking, jostling each other, having a hell of a good time. Then, like thet jaybird had done, one of 'em said something thet sounded just like 'Chrrr! Chrrr! Chrrr!' And, in ten seconds, every Chink around there had disappeared. Man, they raced for the walls of the Black Cow Village like a bunch of chickens. And all the ones thet was on the road outside the dike come tearing over the camel-back bridge, pushing their wheelbarrows and what-all, and the canal coolies thet was towing a barge dropped their towlines and come tearing over the bridge, too. Man, it was the damnedest thing I ever seen. And, along

with everything else, they pulled the kites down, every single
kite."

All had fled, that is, except the mayor of Hai Niu
Cheng. He stood his ground. "Vot hass happened?" asked
Karl Grahlberg. "A band of soldiers is coming in from the
railway tracks," said the mayor quietly. And, just as he said
it, the sentinel on top of the bridge bellowed out, "Armed
party approaching! Armed party approaching!"

Karl roared at his men standing around the hong, "Turn
out der guard! Turn out der damn guard! To me, on der
double!"

The machine gunner and the riflemen on the dike looked
at Karl questioningly. "Shtand fast up dere," he said. "Don'dt

do noddings." He loosened the flap of his pistol holster and strode up over the camel-back bridge. The mayor of the Black Cow Village came with him.

They were Wu Pei-fu's men that were coming in from the railway line. There were about thirty of them—all that were left of a battalion which the Christian general's men had decimated in some bloody sortie out on the plain. They limped along in a blue-gray clot, one donkey cart with pots and blankets on it in their midst. Nearly all of them had been wounded. Nearly all wore bandages. They were dressed in quilted coats, wrapped leggings, and funny little caps brave with the button of Wu Pei-fu. Their average age was between fourteen and eighteen. Their dirty faces were like the faces of lost animals. One officer was with them—a lieutenant. He rode a shaggy little pony, holding its reins in his left hand. His right hand had been chopped off at the wrist.

The column headed straight for the camel-back bridge. When they reached its foot, Karl Grahlberg halted them with upraised hands. With the mayor acting as interpreter, Karl said to the lieutenant, "You are not permitted to pass over this bridge, nor to approach any nearer to the city of Tientsin. You may continue on around Tientsin on the railway track. All the entryways to the city are guarded by international troops, stationed here by treaty with the Chinese government. If you are hungry, I am prepared to feed you. But you must first turn over your arms to me. This is the law."

The lieutenant said something to one of his non-commissioned officers, and the two of them laughed; and the laughter spread through the column of boys. "Vot's so damn funny?" asked Karl.

"Guns," said the mayor. "They think you make the joke."

"I don'dt make no damn choke," said Grahlberg. "Tell

him if he vants to eat, he iss got to gif me some guns. Dot ain'dt no choke."

The mayor spoke again to the lieutenant, and the lieutenant said something to his men. Three of them came up and laid rifles at Karl Grahlberg's feet. They were Czech Mausers, about .28 caliber, long, clumsy, clublike. The stock of one was broken off. The bolt of the second was missing. The third looked as if it might be fired, but the bolt was open and there were no cartridges in its magazine. These were all the arms they had. The lieutenant said something to the mayor. The mayor spoke to Karl Grahlberg. "He asks how much rice these so-dishonored firearms will buy."

"All he can eat, py Gott!" said Karl. "Ve set up a chow line right now. Digby! Get fife more men und bring over der rice!"

Digby Hand and his men came with three big dishpans overflowing, for the sweet-potato man had believed in cooking in quantity. Showing no surprise at all, and acting as if it were an everyday occurrence, the Chinese lieutenant lined up his men, and each came forward with his rice bowl in his hand. Digby Hand served them with a dipper. "Will you have a leg or a wing, sir?" he asked the first little boy. "Lekk? Vink?" said the youngster doubtfully. He wore a bandage around his head. "We'll make it white meat," said Digby, and he filled the boy's bowl with rice. The little soldier looked up at him as if he were God. With one dirty little hand, he touched the raveled edge of the olive drab turtle-neck sweater Digby was wearing. "Hsien hsung," he said. That meant "heaven born."

Karl Grahlberg ordered cabbages brought up and served, too. They were raw, but they were welcome. "Ask der lieutenant," said Karl to the mayor, "iff he vould like tea. I don'dt got none cooked, bot maybe he can cook it, or somedings."

The mayor and the officer parleyed. "He indicates," said

the mayor, "that he would be happy to have tea, and he assures me that he is able to cook it. Also, he says, rather than trouble you for cooked rice, he would accept the raw grain itself. This, he says, is very good rice, but it is not cooked Peking-style, which he prefers."

"Damn dot rice!" said Sergeant Grahlberg. "Giff him two whole sacks. Let him cook it any vay he vants."

"He expresses his thanks," said the mayor. "Now, he will take his men out by the railway and cook and rest."

Toward noon, Captain William B. Tuttle came riding down the dike on Gobi Sun. Karl Grahlberg's machine gunners sat smoking in their sandbagged nest. Karl's riflemen and automatic riflemen snoozed in their foxholes. Karl himself stood on the camel-back bridge, staring at something out toward the railway line. It was the little group of gray-blue-clad Chinese soldiers. Some were making tea; some were sleeping. The atmosphere was pastoral, somnolent. Captain Tuttle's eyes took in the whole scene, but rested mostly on the sturdy sergeant standing on the bridge. Beside the sergeant, leaning against the rail of the bridge, were three battered Czech Mauser rifles. Captain Tuttle looked again at the quiet camp of the casuals and again at Grahlberg. "That sheep may safely graze," said Wild Bill.

Karl Grahlberg saw him and saluted. "Dey is shust liddle boys, sir," he said. "In Shermany, dey vould be in school."

"No trouble with them, eh?" asked Wild Bill.

"No, sir. I didn't need no bullets. Here are deir guns. Dey only had dese t'ree."

"Well, I suppose I'd better talk to their No. 1. Is that him sitting on the pony?"

"Yes, sir. He iss a lieutenant. Vun hand has been shopped off, und it hurts him to lie down. So he shust sit on der pony all der dime."

"Send Jughead down to ask him to come over here. Got any coffee on the stove?"

"Yes, sir."

"Well, lay out some on that table you've got in the hong. I'll receive him there. Draw up a guard and present arms to him when he gets there. Is the mayor around? We'll have him, too. You're to sit in, also. Put a necktie on."

So, in the hong outside the Black Cow Village, on camp chairs around a folding table, there sat down for coffee at noon on October 30, 1924, Captain William B. Tuttle of the 15th U. S. Infantry Regiment, Mayor Li Yang-chang of Hai Niu Cheng, Lieutenant Wei Sho-hsin of Wu Pei-fu's 196th Light Infantry Battalion, and Sergeant Karl Grahlberg, senior duty non-com of E Company of the 15th U. S. Infantry.

Captain Tuttle inquired sympathetically about the lieutenant's severed hand. Didn't he need more medical attention —a better bandaging job, for instance? The lieutenant was puzzled. Bandage hand back on? he asked. How? . . . No, no, said Wild Bill. I meant make stump more comfortable. . . . Comfort? sneered the lieutenant. There was no comfort in war. He banged the stump on the table. This is how I seek comfort, he said.

Wild Bill gave up that line of conversation. Where, he asked, would the lieutenant take his men after they left here? There was a camp available, he pointed out, in the vicinity of Tientsin's Native City, for just such casuals as the lieutenant and his men.

The lieutenant would have none of the camp. He was taking his men to Taku. Field Marshal Wu Pei-fu had transports waiting there to pick up his army, transports and new weapons. The defeat on the plain was nothing. The army of Wu would fight again. The lieutenant pushed his coffee cup aside and stood up. It was a long way to Taku. His men were rested now, and it was time they started off. He thanked the American captain for his hospitality. He bowed, and with his one hand he saluted. Wild Bill stood up and saluted back. "Good luck to you, sir," he said.

Tuttle, the mayor, and Sergeant Grahlberg accompanied the lieutenant as far as the top of the camel-back bridge. There they stood and watched as he ordered his men to prepare to leave. While they were still on the bridge, Lieutenant Colonel Marshall and two of his staff drove up from Tientsin in their brown Dodge touring car, bouncing and slithering over the rutted road.

George Catlett Marshall, in those days, was forty-four years old and possibly the most military-looking man in the entire army. The high-collar tunic worn then, the Sam Browne belt, the flaringly pegged breeches, the boots, the spurs seemed especially designed for him. The corporal on duty at the hong turned out the guard for him and presented arms. Marshall took in the guard, the hong, and the arrangements Sergeant Grahlberg had made there in one sharp glance, then made for the bridge where Wild Bill, Karl, and the mayor were standing. Captain Tuttle and Karl saluted; the mayor bowed. Wild Bill rapidly filled Colonel Marshall in on the situation. As he spoke, the Chinese lieutenant and his little soldiers with the lone donkey cart in their midst began to move off toward the Tientsin-Pukow Railway line. Colonel Marshall stared after them. "More or less the same thing at Dabney's and Burrowes' outguards," he said. "Dabney got eleven rifles. Burrowes got sixteen. This guard setup is working very well. I understand the Japanese had a little trouble somewhere along the Bund. But the Japs always have been trigger-happy." He stared some more at the departing casuals. "I had a better look at them at Dabney's post," he said. "They're awfully young, but that's the way they do things in this country. You could probably make very good soldiers out of them at that. I wouldn't be surprised if some day somebody did."

Then he turned to Karl Grahlberg and said, "You have

handled the situation here very well, Sergeant. Your men are spruced up and alert; your camp is neat and tidy. However, I did notice some flies around the door of the hong. Set up a fly-swatting detail and get rid of them. They might get on your food."

"Yes, sir," said Karl.

Colonel Marshall and his staff rode off in the Dodge, and Wild Bill Tuttle trotted off on Gobi Sun. The field telephone line was brought to the outguard that afternoon. Kites flew high over the Black Cow Village. Canal traffic returned to normal. The two barbers and the sweet-potato seller plied their trades. The villagers, learning from their mayor that Karl's men didn't care much for *tsa-ju*, fetched out bottles of beer instead, which the men cared for very much. For his dinner that night, the villagers brought Karl himself a roast suckling pig, which, because he didn't want to hurt their feelings and because he liked the taste, he devoured bones and all. It was a very tiny pig.

Next morning, Karl set his men to work to tidying up thoroughly around the hong and the field kitchen area. His platoon was to be relieved of outguard duty at noon, when a new platoon from F Company would take its place. Changing of outpost guards was much the same as changing interior guards; everything had to be spick and span, and done with full attention to military detail.

Everything was done by nine o'clock, and Karl's men sat around the hong, smoking and talking. Then one of them noticed that the kites were coming down in the Black Cow Village. There was sort of a stir arising out by the camelback bridge. Karl started off to see what was going on. At that moment, his sentinel on the bridge sang out, "Armed party approaching! Armed party approaching! They're mounted this time, Karl, and, believe me, they're *really* armed."

"I come look," said Karl. "Turn out der guard, Corporal,

und den vait." He trotted to the top of the camel-back bridge.

On big Manchurian ponies, well fed, well shod, well trained, came a troop of horsemen. The troopers' uniforms were of such a dark green that at first glance they looked black. The troopers wore thigh-high, yellow leather boots. Each man carried a lance, the butt of which rested in a leather socket near his left stirrup, the nib of which flaunted itself high over his head and bore a fluttering pennon. Each man at his waist wore a long-barreled Mauser pistol in a wooden holster. Each man also carried a *da bao*, the beheading knife which looks like an oversize machete. These *da baos* were sheathed in canvas scabbards strapped to the troopers' backs. They were unsheathed by the trooper reaching over his shoulder with his right hand, grasping the haft, and jerking the knife free with a flourish. The leader of the troop was an officer with gold braid on his cap and a gold *fourragère* looped over his left shoulder. A pack mule train brought up the rear. Every man in the outfit was a Russian. The unit was a troop of lancers from Chang Tso-lin's Third Eastern Brigade, recruited in Mukden from the White Russian refugees who had fled there after the Bolshevik revolution. These lancers were the elite forces of the warlord of Manchuria.

The kites had all come down in the Black Cow Village. The barbers and the sweet-potato seller and the other hangers-on at the foot of the bridge had scuttled off and disappeared. Traffic on the canal vanished. Karl Grahlberg looked at his machine gun, his automatic riflemen, and his riflemen in their foxholes and behind sandbags on the dike. They made a nice show. It was too bad they had no bullets.

The Mukden lancers halted at a command from their officer. At another command, they drew their Mauser pistols, affixed the grips of them to their wooden holsters which were shaped like rifle stocks, and thus made nasty

little 9 mm. sub-machine guns out of the weapons. They sat
their ponies, lances steadied in left hand, Mausers held in
right hand and rested across the pommel. Back of each
trooper's left ear, the haft of his beheading knife thrust up.
"Dey make a damn goot show," said professional soldier
Karl Grahlberg to his sentinel on the bridge. He started forward to accost them. "Wait, Karl," said a voice behind him.
"Let me get in on the act, too." It was the ubiquitous
Wild Bill Tuttle. With him was the mayor of the Black Cow
Village. "*Mein Gott*, sir, am I gladt to see you!" said the
honest Karl Grahlberg.

"I have only one life to give for my country," said
Wild Bill. "This seems as good a time to offer it as any.
Man, but isn't that a snappy-looking outfit! Come on, Mayor;
let's sally down and meet the lions. You come, too, Karl."

The three of them walked down the slant of the bridge
to the head of the lancer column. The lancer commander
smiled down at Wild Bill, saluted sarcastically, and, in good
English, said, "Good morning, American captain."

Wild Bill did not return the salute. He merely said, "Good
morning. What can we do for you?"

"Oh, probably nothing," said the lancer. "We will water
our horses here, and have breakfast, and then run push on.
This, I believe, is one of those sanctuaries where, under the
protection of American arms, the scum and sweepings of
Wu's army are able to rest and be fed and otherwise ba-
bied."

"We treat 'em all alike," said Wild Bill. "Why don't you
dismount and be *my* guest for breakfast? If your men need
food, we can provide it for them."

"My men need nothing," said the lancer, "but I shall be
honored to be your guest." He gave an order to his troop.
The men wheeled and trotted their ponies toward the spot
where the Chinese casuals had camped the day before. He
dismounted, handed his reins to his orderly, and came up to

Wild Bill with outstretched hand. He was short, heavy-set, and blond. There seemed to be no question but that he was a very competent cavalry leader.

The surprised guards at the hong turned out for him at Karl Grahlberg's order. They presented arms. The hong itself was spotless. Not a fly was to be seen anywhere. The lancer complimented Wild Bill on the appearance of the outguard post. "Beautiful! Beautiful!" he kept saying. At breakfast, hurriedly gotten up by the soldier on mess duty, he put down a plate of corned-beef hash, four poached eggs, two bottles of beer, and four cups of coffee. "You Americans eat off the fat of the land," he said.

He also explained his presence. His lancers were mop-up troops who had taken boat from Shanhaikwan to Taku, had disembarked the night before at that port, and had ridden off long before dawn on a patrol mission across the plain to disarm any Shensi troops that might be found, and make everything safe for the forthcoming arrival of the all-conquering Field Marshal Chang Tso-lin.

"How is it you speak such good English?" asked Wild Bill.

The Russian laughed. "I studied at the Sorbonne. Languages mostly. That was before the revolution. My name is Nesselrode. This lancer idea is my own. I saw the German uhlans parade once. Marshal Chang liked the idea and let me recruit a troop. It's a good outfit. For instance, we could very easily have overrun those guns you have on the dike, in spite of their obvious firepower."

"I wouldn't advise you to try it," said Wild Bill. And then, to change the subject, he said, "Have you done any fighting since you mounted up at Taku?"

"Oh, it was hardly fighting," said the lancer officer. "Just a little group of Wu's men. The only thing they had were sacks of American rice. Their lieutenant had lost a hand, but was still belligerent. The fence posts along the railway line

seemed to need decorating. We put some heads on them."
He laughed.

"Glad you think it's funny," said Wild Bill. "I suppose
you'll be wanting to move out now?"

"Yes," said the Russian. "Always on the move. I've been
on the move all my life. I have enjoyed the breakfast and
the conversation, Captain Tuttle. Look me up the next time
you go to Peking, and I will play the host." He went back
over the camel-back bridge, summoned his troop, and rode
off.

That was the end of the Chihli-Fengtien War, as far as
Karl's outguard was concerned. His platoon was relieved at
noon that day and returned to the American Compound.

On the tenth of November, 1924, Marshal Chang Tso-lin
arrived in Tientsin and took over command of North China.
He made some sort of deal with the Christian General Feng
Yu-hsiang, and peace reigned until 1928 when Chiang Kai-
shek came up from the south and drove Chang back to
Manchuria. In 1938, Chiang himself was driven out of
North China by the Japanese. At the end of the Second
World War, Chiang returned and drove the Japanese out.
A year later, the Chinese Communists under Mao Tse-tung
drove Chiang out. Peace reigns.

In April, 1925, at a ceremony in the American Compound
in Tientsin, the 15th Infantry Regiment was presented with
the marble memorial gate which now stands at Fort Benning,
Georgia. The presentation was made by the mayor of the
Black Cow Village and the mayors of other villages near
which the 15th had set up outguards. The 15th had protected their little villages, and the villagers were grateful.

In 1938, the 15th U. S. Infantry Regiment ended its
twenty-five-year stay in Tientsin and returned to the United
States. The regiment brought its marble gate home with it.
On October 13, 1939, the regiment presented the gate to
the Infantry School at Benning. Captain Philip E. Gallagher

(now Major General, ret.) made the presentation speech. He had been with the 15th as adjutant of the Second Battalion during the outguard days of 1924. In peroration, he said:

"During this period, all the rest of the country, far and near, was ravaged and made desolate. These villagers alone were peaceful and happy. I know of no other case in history where the common people of a country in which a foreign army was stationed ever presented such a memento of their gratitude to that foreign army for protecting them against forces of their own country engaged in civil war."

THE ARMORED TRAIN

9

From 1925 until 1928, things were relatively calm in North China and, hence, positively irenic for the 15th Infantry. Behind the walls of its Compound, the regiment preened and polished and paraded, and practiced the school of the soldier and the school of the squad. Out in the provinces, Chang Tso-lin's beheading knives were busy, but only rarely was the cruel arc of the *da bao* to be seen flashing in Tientsin, and then only in the Native City. Executions were public affairs in those days, but the Native City was quite a distance from the American Compound, and few members of the regiment ever attended the decapitation ceremonies. The official photographer for our regiment—a Chinese cameraman of Steichen-like artistry—never missed a single one, however. He was a regular Boswell in his love of watching capital punishment being administered. He took some remarkable pictures. In one, he caught the exact moment of the severance: the head in the air; the headless body, arms bound, still kneeling; the tip of the *da bao* chipping into the pavement as its downward stroke is ended. The face of the executioner has a more agonized look on it than does the face of the victim, but there is a unity in the two faces—as if, at that same instant, both were looking into the mouth of hell. I bought a copy of the picture and showed it to Digby Hand. "Yeah," he said, "I've seen it already. Gonna send it home to your old folks?"

"No," I said, "but I might take it home as a souvenir. It sort of symbolizes something—the Chinks in their native village whacking off heads, and us here in the Compound going to movies in the Recreation Hall, eating frog legs and veal cutlets, drinking beer. This is their country, you know."

"So what?" asked Digby.

I had no answer to that.

Corporal Moody Henlaw came up. I showed him the picture. "Yeah," he said. "I seen it already." He had been in the army nine years and, in between two of his hitches, had served as a deputy sheriff in some county of Oklahoma. Everyone, naturally, called him "Sheriff."

He took the picture from me and looked at it some more. "It ain't human to do it like thet," he said. "Back in Okly-homy I remember onct, there was this fella—Big Red—

and he up and kilt his wife and his pappy-in-law and another fella. Some sort of family trouble they was having. They was Indians and lived on the reservation. Well, he ended the family trouble all right, and then he come around and turned hisself in to me. Easiest doggone arrest I ever made. The papers was full of it, pitchers of me and Big Red and Red's wife and ever'body. Well, they tried Big Red and found him guilty—not a hell of a lot else they could of done—and they said to execute him. The federal government tried him 'cause he lived on a reservation and was a ward of the government, and the government had to execute him right there on the reservation, 'cause thet was the law; and so the whole thing got turned over to the U.S. marshal. We hung 'em in Oklyhomy in those days when we had to execute 'em—none of this chopping off heads like the Chinks here do.

"Hell of it was, the U.S. marshal was new on the job—just thet month got appointed to office—and he didn't know hair ner hide about hanging anybody. So he called on the sheriff's office to give him a hand. Well, we didn't know nothing about hanging, neither. Course, we'd all been to lynchings and things like that, but I mean legal hanging. So the U.S. marshal called in a professional guy from Texas to do the job. This Texan contracted to put up the scaffold on the Indian reservation and everything. And he did. He was a mighty neat carpenter. And when he up and showed us how to tie a hangman's noose, why you jest *knew* he really savvied his business. But he was a drinking man, and there was where the trouble come in. The U.S. marshal had deppitized all us guys in the sheriff's office as deppity U.S. marshals so's we could come along to the hanging and act as guards in case the Indians acted up. Turned out he didn't need no guards at all; nothing like thet happened.

"We got Big Red up on the scaffold—no trouble there, Red was as do-cyle as a lamb—and this Texas hangman puts

the rope around his neck. It was then thet we see thet the
Texan is drunk. But there ain't nothing we can do about it.
Well, he horsed around a while—a damn long while—making adjustments and things, until finally the U.S. marshal
got sore and said, 'Fer God's sake, get going with it!' So
the Texan says, 'You fellas in Oklyhomy is always wanting
action. Well, stand back, Marshal, and you'll see how a
Texican *gits* action.'

"Then, 'stead of pulling the trigger on the trap like he
was s'posed to do, he just hauls off and kicks loose the plank
Big Red is standing on. Down comes Red—his hands is tied,
of course, and he's got a sack over his head—and he jest
kind of hangs there, halfway through the trap door. The
court order said to hang him by the neck till he was dead,
but the U.S. marshal was a mighty humane man. He seen
what had happened and he could hear pore Red choking
and gasping. So he says, 'Damn the court order,' and he takes
out his thirty-eight-forty and puts Red out of his misery. I
reckon if sech a thing was to happen here in China, the
Chinks would jest let the man hang there and suffer till he
starved to death. Hell, if we'd tried to chop off Big Red's
head in Oklyhomy like they're always doing here in Tientsin,
they'd of run us out of office so quick you couldn't of said
scat."

"Thet's all very true," said Digby Hand. "But if you
was to ask me, Sheriff, they ain't much difference in the
long run. The only thing is the Chinks seem to do it
quicker and neater in the Native City than you birds done
it back in Oklyhomy."

"We was law officers," said the Sheriff. "We was paid to
do our job."

"Well, if they'd of given you a *da bao* instead of a rope,
would you have done the job *thet* way?" asked Digby.

"I reckon," said the Sheriff. "When a man's swore in, he
expects to do his job.

"The beheading knife," he continued, looking at the picture again, "is definitely not a white man's instermunt. I had a good look at them Russkie lancers thet come up to Karl Grahlberg's outguard thet time back in '24. You remember 'em, Digby; you was there, too. Anyhow, I had a good look at them Russkies, and I says to myself, 'I betcha you jokers ain't in the same league with the Chinks when it comes to swinging them things.' I says to myself, 'Likely the Chinks has been swinging them big knives fer centuries and has got the hang of it, but you Russkies wouldn't know how to use 'em fer shucks.' Thet's what I said."

"They used 'em all right on thet little gang of Chinks we fed the rice to," said Digby. "I seen the pictures of those kids' heads on the fence poles. Don't tell me those Russkies don't savvy the *da bao*. I seen the proof."

"Hit says in the Bible," said the Sheriff, "thet them as lives by the sword shall die by the sword. I wouldn't want to be no Russkie soldier in this man's country."

Early in 1928, Field Marshal Chang Tso-lin, warlord of Manchuria and ruler in fact of North China, looked south from Peking, his capital by right of possession, and noted the approach of General Chiang Kai-shek, commander of the Chinese Nationalist armies and strong right arm of the Kuomintang, the dominant Chinese political party. In the four years since the incidents at the Black Cow Village, Chiang had consolidated his hold on South China and was now moving north in amoeba-like fashion to have it out with Chang Tso-lin.

Chang counted heads, concluded that Chiang's forces were superior to his own, and, rather than risk a Cannae at Peking, decided to pull his troops not only out of that city but out of North China in general and take refuge behind the Great Wall from whence he had come originally.

He took all the rolling stock on the Peking-Mukden

Railway with him when he made his exodus, so that unless he brought rolling stock with him Chiang would not be able to pursue the Mukden armies by rail. That rolling stock, everything from deluxe *wagon-lits* to coaches, cabooses, gondolas, locomotives, switch engines, and all else on wheels poured for days down the railway from Peking through Tientsin, bearing Chang's blue-clad men back to Manchuria. We used to stand on the viaduct at Tientsin East and watch the rivers of men flow on slow currents of wheels through the yards and on out of the city. Since then, whenever at dusk I see trains moving, I always recall those times we stood on the viaduct. For me, it symbolizes loneliness. When the movement was over, not even a handcar remained on some six or seven hundred miles of track. Chang Tso-lin had left only a small holding force behind him in Peking to delay the advance guards of the Kuomintang.

On June 8, 1928, the great pullout ended, and so did the personal history of Field Marshal Chang Tso-lin. He had reserved for himself the last passenger train to leave Peking, as does a good leader who follows up his retrograding troops to see that everything is being done in shipshape order. On the approaches to Mukden, far inside the so-called safety of the Great Wall, his train was blown up with land mines, and so was he. His son, the Young Marshal, Chiang Hsueh-liang, took over. Everybody said the Japanese had blown up Old Chang, but nobody ever proved it.

Joseph W. Stilwell, a major in those days, was the 15th Infantry's expert on all things Chinese—political, economic, and military. It was the custom for the regiment to assemble once a month in the Recreation Hall for a briefing by Major Stilwell on the Chinese situation. He was a brilliant, incisive speaker; his knowledge of the maze that was North China was impressive.

Two days after Sheriff Moody Henlaw's discourse on beheading knives and executions in Oklahoma and in general, the regiment assembled in the Recreation Hall for a briefing. On the platform with Stilwell sat Colonel Isaac Newell, then regimental commander.

Major Stilwell told us how, in the great wedge of land formed by Peking, Tientsin, and Shanhaikwan, there existed a vacuum. Chang Tso-lin's forces were out, and Chang himself was dead. Chiang Kai-shek's troops had not yet arrived in sufficient numbers to impose order. Lawlessness stalked in the wedge again as it had in the days of 1924. So, it looked as if it would be back to roadblocks and the outguards for the 15th. The Peking-Mukden Railway, denuded of its rolling stock, posed a special problem. The telephone and telegraph lines had been torn down. It was impossible to know what was going on, except in the immediate area of Tientsin. Some enterprising Chinese general conceivably might scrape together enough coal cars and an engine or two in the hinterlands to make up troop trains and swoop down upon Tientsin, set up shop, and announce himself as ruler of North China. There was the question of recognition. The United States government recognized the government of Nationalist China. But it had also recognized the *de facto* rule of Chang Tso-lin. The practice, indeed, was to recognize whoever happened to be on the spot, but not to the point of taking sides. If a warlord moved into Tientsin, and claimed it, he would probably be recognized now. A token force would do the trick, because all the Manchurians had left. But when Chiang Kai-shek and his Nationalists reached Tientsin and proposed to battle it out with this hypothetical warlord—then what? Take sides, or fight them both? These things, said Stilwell cynically, were still being pondered in the diplomatic realm where the wheels of the gods ground so slowly that what grist they did produce was imperceptible, if any. At any rate, he said, there was no intention *at present* for the United States Army Forces in China to fight Chiang Kai-shek's wars for him.

Stilwell let it go at that, and Colonel Newell stood up. Tall, gray-haired, dignified, all army through and through, he was probably the most beloved commander the regiment ever had in its China days. He had an odd little habit of rolling his own cigarettes, using brown paper. We used to joke about it.

He was just as good a speaker as Stilwell. He thanked him for his summation of the situation, and then brought the matter down to its practical basis. Tientsin East, the huge railway center, was considered the hub of the situation. If anything came in on rails, it would wind up there. The international forces in Tientsin would want to know immediately when it got there and what it was and what its intentions were.

So, in order that all the international commands would know at the *same time* what was happening, an international guard would be formed and stationed at Tientsin East. It would be small. Its mission would be to observe and report. An international command center would be set up at Gordon Hall in the British Concession, and appropriate telephone connections would be cut through to the international guard at Tientsin East. This guard was not to pick fights or throw its weight around. Immediate command of the guard would rotate alphabetically between the powers. Thus, an American officer would command the first detail, a Britisher the next, a Frenchman the next, an Italian the next, and a Japanese the last.

This international guard would demonstrate that all the occupying nations of Tientsin had an interest in the matter, said Colonel Newell. There would be a stand of five flags. There would be a contrast of uniforms and arms. There would be a showing forth of unity. The members of the guard would be specially picked men. They would carry live ammunition.

Specially picked. Well, I suppose they were. E Company, the leadoff company of the regiment, was ordered to furnish a corporal and two privates to make up the United States of America's share in the first international detail. Everything was done by rotation in those days, and E Company, being at the top of the regimental list alphabetically, invariably got in first on everything that happened. So Karl Grahlberg, hero of the Black Cow Village affair of 1924, senior duty sergeant and acting first sergeant in place of the regular top kick, who was temporarily on the sick list, was ordered to assign a corporal and two privates to the detail. Karl consulted the duty roster. The Sheriff, Moody Henlaw, was the next corporal up for guard duty. Digby Hand and myself were the next privates. Karl Grahlberg spoke to the Sheriff, and the Sheriff spoke to us.

"C'mon, you guys. Full pack. Rifles, bayonets, tin hats. Shirts 'n' ties. Here's yer ammunition. Let's go."

Thus, the specially picked detail was formed. It went by jinrikishas to Tientsin East, the Sheriff's conveyance leading the way. Behind us came two more jinrikishas, bearing our bedding, our Springfield rifles, and our packs. It was the only way to get there unless we walked, for the 15th's motor pool consisted only of the commander-in-chief's Cadillac, two Dodge touring cars which Headquarters used, and three White trucks which would not run. Service Company's mule-drawn forage wagons were deemed too unwieldy for our present mission.

We made it to Tientsin East in good time, for our jinrikisha pullers were swift, sturdy men. The American lieutenant, a British, a French, an Italian, and a Japanese officer were at the station when we got there. They had made arrangements with the depot officials for housing and catering to the international guard, and all was in readiness for us when we disenjinrikishaed.

Our officer, a lieutenant we didn't know very well because he had spent most of his time at the Language School in Peking, scowled at the Sheriff, and said, "It's about time you got here." He showed us the place where he and the other officers had decided to station the guard. It was a roofed but otherwise open-air loading platform at the end of the depot proper. Marked out with chalk was the spot where the machine gun, which the British would supply, would be set up. Marked out were positions for sandbags, and the spot where the stand of five flags would be placed. There was a restroom for us to use in the depot. There was a special telephone booth. Everywhere we went, a flock of Chinese onlookers came along, too. Beggars showed up by the dozens. The Japanese officer snarled something at them, and they vanished. "Thet's a speech I'd like to learn," said Digby Hand in admiration of the Jap's blazing epithets. "Hit's only one Oriental cussing out anothern," said Sheriff Henlaw. "No white man has got the meanness of sperit to use thet kind of talk."

The Britishers, two machine gunners from the Welsh Border Regiment, came along, carrying their weapon between them, their duffel slung over their shoulders. The gun was a mean-looking .303 Maxim, water-cooled, mounted on a tripod. Each gunner also carried a .450 Webley service revolver in a waist holster. By the time they had their Maxim set up to suit them and their lieutenant, the remainder of the international guard had assembled; two Italian marines, armed with little pistols and big rifles, dressed in their weird half-soldier, half-sailor uniforms; two bearded French artillerymen armed with Lebel carbines; and two Japanese infantrymen lugging Arisaki rifles almost as long as the Japs themselves were tall. All of us except the Nipponese wore steel helmets. They wore garrison caps.

There was an informal presentation of each other's troops by the various officers, then an argument between those officers as to which flag should occupy the position of honor in the center of the flag rack. It was decided to use the alphabetical system again: the American flag in the center spot the first day, the British the next, and so on. The Japanese officer—a major (everytime anything of the sort happened, the Japs always made sure that their man held the highest rank)—objected violently that this alphabet business always condemned Japan to bring up the rear; but the British, French, and Italian lieutenants joined ours in shouting him down. "Thet there is the only way to do it," said the Sheriff. "Jest holler and point; the one thet hollers loudest and points hardest wins. You don't need no interpreter ner nothing thet way. Hit's the way we used to settle things with the Indians of Oklyhomy. It works with these here Orientals, too."

We brought benches down from the depot waiting room and arranged them in a semicircle around the Maxim machine gun, the focal point of the international detail. We mounted guard by sitting down on the benches, Americans on one bench, British on the next, and so on—alphabetically, of course.

The officers held a final huddle, then, leaving our lieutenant in command, saluted and dispersed. "Well," said Digby Hand, "what do we do now, Sheriff? Jest sit?"

"I reckon," said the Sheriff, "unless the lieutenant thinks up something he wants did. What's wrong with setting?"

"Nothing," said Digby. "Only I know now how a goldfish feels." All around our semicircle Chinese had gathered and were staring at us impassively, indeed almost incuriously. There was nothing else in or around the depot to stare at, so they gathered and stared at us.

Our lieutenant came back from saying good-by to the other officers, looked us over, and bit his lip. Finally, he said, "This is a damned silly situation. I don't think the practicality of it was properly assessed. But I suppose there's nothing for it but just *to* sit. Obviously, there are no posts to walk. There's nothing to guard either, for that matter. If anything does come along the tracks, you'll be able to see it from here as well as from anyplace else, and I suppose that's the crux of the matter. You men can smoke. I'm going to the depot and report in over the phone. Take over, Corporal Henlaw. If anything happens, let me know."

It was very boring. The Italians and the French seemed to understand one another and began to discuss something which seemed very hilarious to them. The Japanese made absolutely no conversation at all. I tried to strike up some talk with the Welsh Borderers: "How much time do you chaps still have to do in China?" "Eh?" one of them said, when it finally dawned on him I was speaking to him. I repeated my question. He looked at his comrade. The comrade shrugged. "Unt knaow," he said. "This here is all very peaceful and restful," said Digby Hand, "but my laigs is getting stiff. Is there anything in the orders, Sheriff, that says I mustn't git up and stretch 'em a bit?"

"I reckon not," said the Sheriff, "but don't go straying off too far. The lieutenant's liable to be back any time, and if he seed you wasn't here, he'd be liable to swear. Hit's a mighty bad thing fer a man to swear. Sa'nter down to the end of the platform, Digby, and see if they is any trains coming. That'll give you a chance to stretch yer laigs in line of duty."

"Thank yuh, Sheriff," said Digby. "I always knew you had the welfare of yer men at heart." He made his way through the surrounding Chinese, ambled down the platform, and disappeared behind some tall bins which cut off our view of the tracks. He came back on the double. "By God," he said, "there *is* a train coming! Damnedest looking thing you ever seen."

Even the Japanese could tell something was happening. As a body, the international guard rose to its feet, moved out to the edge of the platform, and peered down the rails.

The lieutenant came back from his telephone call. "What the hell's going on?" he wanted to know. "Some sort of catawampus coming down the track, sir," said the Sheriff. "Nonsense," said the lieutenant, and thrust himself between us to have a look.

It was a catawampus all right, the first of its kind we had ever seen. On a flatcar, coming straight toward us, seemingly with its muzzle pointed down our throats, was a rapid-firing naval cannon of about three-inch bore. Behind it came two boxcars, plated with armor and mounting machine guns in top and side turrets. Then came the locomotive, so covered with armor that it was recognizable only by its smokestack. The locomotive was followed by two more armor-plated, turreted boxcars. A flatcar, mounting another artillery piece, brought up the rear. The catawampus looked like some weirdly misshapen naval vessel of the destroyer class.

Cars and locomotives were camouflaged with long, wavy lines of gray and yellow and brown. One of the boxcars— apparently the command car—was additionally decorated with big cartoons. The first in the sequence showed a series of flags—British, French, American, Japanese, Russian, Italian. Across them was painted a yellow slash. That symbolized China's superiority. The second cartoon depicted a big Chinese soldier flourishing rifle and bayonet and chasing a group of midget soldiers dressed in foreign uniforms. That symbolized China's cleaning house. The last cartoon was a picture of a big Chinese civilian lying on his back, bleeding from many atrocious wounds. Lapping up his blood were Japanese and Europeans and Americans. That symbolized China's grievance. From a staff on the command car, the Nationalist flag of China flew.

The armor of the train was pitted from many bullet impacts. But none of the bullets had penetrated. "Yessir," said the Sheriff, "thet there's a real catawampus."

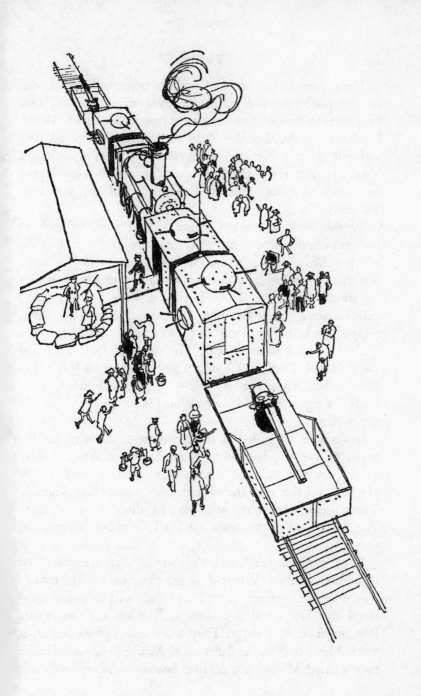

The armored train stopped with its command car parallel to our platform. We could see eyes staring at us from peepholes in the car. Our lieutenant tapped one of the Welsh Borderers on the shoulder. "Go and call the command post and tell them a Nationalist armored train has pulled into Tientsin East. Keep the line open for a follow-up report from me. Be quick about it." "Yessir," said the Borderer, and trotted off.

By this time so many Chinese had gathered to look at the catawampus that some of them were even standing on our benches. A door in the command car opened; a ramp was shoved out, bridging the car with the platform on which we stood. An officer strode forth. He wore a green tunic, yellow riding breeches with red stripes down the sides, sloppy black leather boots that came up to his knees, and a silver-braided forager's cap. His shoulder boards carried the gold and silver insigne of a major. He wore a black Sam Browne belt; from the left side of it a cavalry saber hung; from the right side a Mauser pistol. He smoked a cigar. He was a Russian.

In Chinese, he yelled at the crowd to make way, to disperse, to get the hell away from his train. An impassive silence was the only response. "Hey, Sheriff," said Digby Hand, "ain't thet guy the same damn Russkie that Wild Bill Tuttle made chop-chop with at the Black Cow Village? You know, when we were on Karl Grahlberg's outguard there?"

"The resemblance," said the Sheriff, "is oncanny. But he had hosses then. Where'd he get this here tin-can train?"

The Russian officer turned and bellowed into his command car. Out came five soldiers, Russians also, short and lean and incredibly dirty. They wore soiled green uniforms, scarred leather boots, and flat caps. As did their commander, they carried Mauser pistols, but, instead of sabers, each was also armed with a heavy Chinese beheading knife, the fearsome *da bao*.

"Hit's the same outfit, Digby," said the Sheriff. "Old Chang Tso-lin's head-whackers. Only I don't get this Nationalist flag they're flying. They was on the other side the last time we seen 'em."

The major gave a new, more threatening order to the crowd; his men unsheathed their *da baos*. The Chinese complained loudly, but backed away from him and his warriors. Those who had been standing on our benches stepped down and shuffled aside.

Our lieutenant confronted the Russian. "What's all this knife-waving about?" he asked angrily. "Or, do you speak English? This area is under international guard, you know."

"So I perceive," said the major, looking us over. "Yes, I speak English. My intent is not pugnacious. Coal and water I need for my train. So I stop here to make the arrangement. I will sign chits on the Kuomintang for everything." He laughed. "I do not believe I met you, Lieutenant, when I brought my lancers through this 'area,' as you describe it, four years ago. It was a captain, I believe, who was then so amiable of an host. But, now, I am in a position to act as host. May I invite you, sir, to board my train and have tea, and discuss the situation? You will find my private car well equipped. In addition, it is safe." And, with his saber, he tapped on the armor plating and laughed.

"All right," said our lieutenant. "I'll have a cup of tea with you. I have already reported your arrival here, you know. If you try anything funny, we'll throw a switch on your train and let the French artillery blast it off the tracks."

"Well," said the major, "I have a great respect for French artillery. Just to show there should be no distrust between us, I will leave a hostage with your men while you and I have tea. He speaks English and is a very valuable man. He is of your rank—a lieutenant."

He gave an order in Russian; it was relayed inside the armored car, and a lieutenant appeared. He, like the major, was blond and heavy-set, but he wore no sidearms. "Lieutenant Bilski," said the major. "He will wait with your men. Come, sir," and he bowed our lieutenant into his car.

Lieutenant Bilski grinned, sat down on one of our benches, and said, "Murrcan cigarette I tink I like." The Sheriff didn't smoke, so I gave him one. "Dank oo," said Bilski.

"Bloody Yank show like always," said one of the Welsh Borderers. "Wot the 'ell they want us 'ere for, anyhow?" The two French soldiers and the two Italian marines stared at the Russian guards at the door of the armored car and managed to start a conversation with them in some sort of intermediate language. It apparently was salacious, because both sides did a lot of laughing and gesturing. The two Japanese grunted quietly between themselves. One of them made some notes in a little notebook.

"Well," said the Sheriff companionably to Lieutenant Bilski, "I reckon hit's been mighty adventuresome, comporting yerselfs around in this here catawampus. 'Pears like you've had to contest yore passageway somewhurs er other. *Comprend?*"

"No understand," said Bilski, inhaling on his cigarette.

"He means," said Digby Hand, "how is it you guys got this train in the first place and how come it's flying the Chinese Nationalist flag? You guys ain't Nationalists, are you?"

"Steal train," said Bilski. "Steal flag. Steal ever' damn t'ing. Now ve go home."

"Where's home?" asked Digby.

"Mukden."

"The war's over, huh?"

"Ofer? No. No ofer. Var neffer ofer. Alvays var."

"Nice thought," said Digby. "Tell us how you stole the train."

"Chinoise drunk," said Bilski. "Ve shoot, ve chop. Now go back to Mukden. Fife years no see Mukden."

"They's no place like home," said the Sheriff.

"Mukden not home. Kharkov iss home. But no more."

"Whatcha been doing fer women?" asked the Sheriff.

"Ve see. Ve take." Bilski waved his hand. "Many men sick. I sick. Too many sick vomen ve take."

"You better get on the needle quick as you can," said Digby.

"I hear tell," said the Sheriff, "thet venereal diseases ain't so hard on Rooshians. They hardly think nothing about it. They're like the Chinks thataway."

"No understand," said Bilski.

"'E cawn't even understand the ruddy syph. Coo, wot a bloke!" snorted the larger of the two Welsh Borderers.

Lieutenant Bilski stared him straight in the face. "Insult?" he asked sharply.

"No, hit wasn't no insult, Lieutenant," said the Sheriff firmly. "Hit was jest iggerant comment from an iggerant person." And to the Borderer he said, "You keep yer mouth shet hereafter, unless yer spoke to first."

"I'll bloody well speak when I bloody well please, Yank," said the Borderer.

"And I'll bloody well stomp yer yeller teeth in if you try it," said the Sheriff.

It looked as if we might have a real fight there on that loading platform at Tientsin East, a fight between an American corporal and a British private. The onlookers would be one more British private, two American privates, two French, two Italian, two Japanese privates, five White Russian guards and their officer, Lieutenant Bilski, and all the Chinese civilians who were crowded onto the platform. The Sheriff was a big man, and so was the Welsh Borderer. It would have been a good fight, and everybody would have enjoyed it.

But it didn't happen. Our lieutenant came out of the armored car, accompanied by the Russian major. They spoke
in undertones; the major and Bilski and the train guards returned to their car; the ramp was drawn in; the door closed.
Some kind of signal was given, and the armored train
chugged down the track. We looked at our lieutenant.

"Everything's in order," he said. "That is, as near to being
in order as anything can be in this cockeyed country.
That train is their spoils of war. They're just passing
through. They'll coal and water down in the yards and keep
on going. It's none of our affair. We're not taking sides in
this war. I'm going to the telephone to report. You men
stand easy." He left.

Said the Welsh Borderer to the Sheriff, "Ah'll fight yer
rahght now, chap."

"We'll hafta make it later," said the Sheriff regretfully.
"I cain't do no fighting while I'm on duty. How about
outside yer Union Jack Club come next Monday night?"

"Our bloody MPs'd stop it," said the Borderer. "'Ow
'bout at yer Sergeants' Club?"

"Thet'll be fine," said the Sheriff. They shook hands on
it.

Our detail was relieved from international guard the next
day, and replaced by another unit. In a short while we
heard more about the White Russians in the armored train.
We heard about them in the Blue Compound, where many
of Tientsin's White Russians lived. Gus Krites was back in
the Blue Compound, between fur-buying trips which the
war had interrupted. He and Polya were living with her
mother. Digby and I paid them a visit. We asked Gus if he
had heard anything about the armored train. "Damn near
all I do hear any more," he said.

Two of the Russians on the train had "jumped ship" in
Tientsin; another below Taku. They had found refuge in

the Blue Compound, and from them Gus had heard all about the train.

"It was the damnedest thing," said Krites. "It was the damnedest thing."

Chang Tso-lin had left his Mukden lancers behind in Peking to cover his retreat. They had covered it all right, but when it was over there was no way for them to get back . . . unless they rode their horses all the way from Peking to Mukden. This, their major was prepared to do . . . until he heard of the Nationalist armored train which had just reached Peking. He decided to highjack it and use it for his private transportation. The Chinese from the south who were manning it didn't know exactly where they were in the Peking yards, and it was easy for the Russians to throw a switch and signal the slowly moving train off on a dead-end spur. Then the Russians, with their major doing the talking, presented themselves as a sort of welcoming committee, dissidents who had defected from the Fengtien army, and coaxed the Chinese out of their armored shell with sweet talk of wine, women, and song. It was night, and it was lonely in the railway yards. Chang Tso-lin had long since emptied them. Once the Chinese were out of their train, the Russians went to work with their *da baos*. *Da baos* make no noise.

Then the Russians took over the train. Some of them had worked on railways before and knew how to operate the locomotive. They left Peking in a hurry. They kept the Nationalist flag flying on the locomotive's staff as a safety measure.

Instead of barreling straight through to Manchuria on the Peking-Mukden Railway, they coursed around on the lines that fan out from Peking, trying to find if there were any pockets of Fengtien troops left which they might pick up and take along with them. There was nothing to stop them. Communication lines were down; there was no other rolling stock on the steel rails. They lived off the country. Any time they wanted anything, they would stop at the nearest Chinese village, train their cannon on the village, and take it. Food, coal, wine, women—anything they saw and wanted, they took. "Jest like old Quantrill did in the Civil War," said Digby Hand admiringly.

Their major finally decided to get back to Manchuria while the tracks were still open. Chiang Kai-shek would have been certain to have heard of his train's loss by now, and would be determined to do something about it. Fun was fun, and raping little defenseless villages was fun, but the hourglass was running out.

So the armored train headed down the Peking-Mukden line for Manchuria. When it stopped at Tientsin East to take on coal and water, there was our international guard staring at it.

Two of the Russian soldiers on it quietly deserted while their major was talking to our lieutenant, and while we were talking to their Lieutenant Bilski. They made their way to the Blue Compound, where they had friends and relatives. The third one deserted at Taku, and came up to Tientsin on foot, where he, too, found his way to the Blue Compound. He was in pretty bad shape from a bullet wound.

The railway at Taku passes close to the docking area where the Hai Ho spews out into the gulf and builds up Taku Bar, where the deep-draft vessels must anchor. But smaller vessels can steam right over Taku Bar and go all the way up the Hai to Tientsin if they care to. A smaller vessel *had* steamed over Taku Bar and was idling at the docks when the purloined armored train came down the track. It was a Chinese Nationalist gunboat, and its quick-firing cannon knocked out the armored locomotive, blew the artillery pieces off the flatcars, and riddled the armored boxcars almost before the White Russians knew where the

barrage was coming from. A Nationalist transport had unloaded its men from Taku Bar; they mopped up what needed
mopping after the gunboat ceased firing.

In a week or so, some pictures reached Tientsin from
Taku. Our regimental photographer secured negatives of
them and printed his own glossies to offer for sale. One of
them which I bought was remarkably clear. It showed a
telephone pole festooned with heads. On the peak of the
pole—the position of honor, I suppose—was the head of the
White Russian major, still brave in its gold-braided cap.

I took the picture back to the Compound and showed it
to Digby Hand. "Yeah," he said. "I seen it already." We
were standing in front of the Memorial Gate which the
villagers had presented to the 15th back in 1925. Sheriff
Moody Henlaw came along, and I showed the picture to
him. "Yeah," he said. "I seen it already." He still had a
puffy bruise on his cheek where the Welsh Borderer had
hit him during their fight, a fight which had ended in a
draw and with both of them getting very drunk afterward
in the Sergeants' Club.

"I seen it already," he said. "But lemme see it ag'in." He
took it and studied it a while. "You know, Digby, we seen
them Russkies at Black Cow Village, and we seen them little
Chinks they beheaded. We seen them Russkies ag'in at Tientsin East. Now here their haids are on a pole like them little
Chinks' haids was. But what I cain't figger, Digby, is what
the hell all the fightin' was about."

THE MARINES LAND

10 ❊

In the summer of 1928, some time after the armored train incident, there was formed in the Peking-Tientsin-Shanhaikwan area what was known as the Northern Coalition. It consisted of a triumvirate of field marshals named Sun Chuan-fang, Chang Tsung-chang, and Chang Hsueh-liang, the last being the son of the defunct warlord Chang Tso-lin and the inheritor of the rule over Manchuria. The aim of the Northern Coalition was to balk Chiang Kai-shek, whose own aim was the control of all China under the aegis of the Kuomintang. Large armies were arrayed on both sides. Diplomats of the foreign powers in China, gloomily foreseeing all-out war at last, decided that their own forces had better be strengthened, and hurriedly so. This man, Chiang Kai-shek, leader of the Chinese National-ists, evidently meant business.

So the British brought in more men, and the French

brought in more men, and the Italians brought in more men, and so did the Japanese and the Americans.

The Japanese brought in more men than anybody else, and formed what was later to become known in World War II as the Kwangtung Army. The United States brought in the Fourth Brigade of Marines—four thousand men— under Brigadier General Smedley Butler, and stationed them in and around Tientsin. Soon the foreign troops in North China, from Peking to the sea, numbered about twelve thousand. They were scattered, and command, of course, was incredibly divided, but they made a potent force.

In our dayrooms, at our mess tables, on practice marches, and over beers in the bars around our Compound, we of the 15th Infantry discussed the marines and their coming. Most of us had never seen a leatherneck. But one, Corporal Fautz, had served a whole four-year cruise as a marine. To him we directed most of our questions. He was very proud of the globe and anchor. "A first-class private in the Gyrenes," he said, "has got to know more—a hell of a lot more—than a second lieutenant in this lint-picking outfit. And as fer officers, well, one of our lieutenant colonels wouldn't make a pimple on the nose of a leatherneck shavetail."

"Ah hell," said little Calhoun Shaw, "that's a lot of baloney, Fautz, and you know it. They take the flunk-outs from Annapolis and West Point and wait till their class graduates, and then make marine lieutenants out of them. They ain't so damned good; they're jest culls. I got an uncle what's a gunnery sergeant in the marines—he told me all about their damned officers. That's why I joined the infantry."

"Well, thet uncle of yours oughta be court-martialed fer talking thet way," said Fautz. "It's a damn lie in the first place; those gunnery sergeants got espree dee corpse. They don't go around talking thet way about their officers."

"Like hell they don't," said little Shaw.

These conversations, and similar ones, served to build up our curiosity about the sea-soldiers to a high degree. When word came that the marines would start landing the next evening along Tientsin's Bund, practically all of us who would not be on duty made a vow to be there and watch them at it. However, when the next evening arrived, some sort of an alert had been sounded in the meantime from the Native City, and the Third Battalion was restricted to the Compound under combat readiness, and the Second Battalion was ordered to be back in the Compound under a 10 P.M. curfew. We were warned that if we did go to the Bund to watch the marines, we were to behave ourselves and not indulge in any hoodlumism.

Digby Hand, Martin Lord, and I decided we could abide by those restrictions, and, immediately after supper, which was served at 5 P.M., took off for the Bund in jinrikishas. The marines were coming up the Hai Ho on lighters and barges from their transports which were moored at Taku Bar. There was still no rolling stock available on the Peking-Mukden Railway.

The Bund, as usual, was teeming. And, as usual, a Japanese destroyer was tied up below the swinging berth. A gangplank had been put out to shore, and the gangplank was guarded by four Jap sailors. Digby Hand waved and spoke civilly to them as we passed, but they stood immobile and said nothing. "The life of a Jap sailor does not seem to be too happy a one," said Martin Lord. "They feed 'em on seaweed and keelhaul 'em at the drop of a kimono. Banzai to all that, I say."

We noticed a small group of our own officers standing at a vantage spot on the Bund, and we drew up behind them to hear what they were talking about. They were discussing the marines. They discussed them from various angles, and finally one of the officers, a Headquarters man, said, "If

you ask me, I think they're just a bunch of b.s. publicity."
The others seemed to concur.

A tug brought up the first three lighters of marines and
lodged them, with much banging and clattering, against the
concrete rim of the Bund. Lines were thrown ashore and
made fast. The lighters were aswarm with young Americans
in forest-green uniforms, very dirty, very disheveled. Each
man wore a steel helmet and carried a pack, a horseshoe-
shaped blanket roll, a Springfield rifle with bayonet fixed, a
cartridge belt jammed with shiny .30-06 ammunition clips,
and an extra bandolier of cartridges over his shoulder. "Man,
these guys're really loaded for big game," said Digby Hand.
"Makes me think of the time at the Black Cow Village
when we carried wooden plugs in our cartridge belts."

The three lighter loads of marines emptied onto the Bund;
there was nothing to stop them. They had only to leap
ashore; the lighters were parallel to and tied to the concrete ramp. The Chinese civilians maintained a wary distance. Even we of the 15th Infantry backed away from their
determined enterprise. Out of the bowels of their lighters—
which had been previously used for transporting coal, and
hence were rather sooty—the landing parties hoisted machine
guns, Stokes mortars, and 27 mm. howitzers. They did it
quickly, efficiently, seemingly without effort, as do well-
trained teams. They brought out sandbags; and in something
like ten minutes they threw up a horseshoe-shaped barricade,
facing the city and sealing off their portion of the Bund.
This barricade bristled with weapons.

Martin Lord said, "Maybe somebody ought to tell them
that the war hasn't exactly started yet."

We moved over closer to get a better look at them. We
wore our usual street dress: roll-collar tunics, white shirts,
black ties, Pershing caps with patent-leather visors, gleaming "Can-Do's" on our lapels. Our slacks were pressed, our

leather belts and shoes shiny as mirrors. We carried swagger sticks.

The tunic the marines wore was the high-collar World War I model with black buttons. Their pants were stuffed into canvas leggings. Half the legging straps which went under the marines' insteps were broken and flopped around and, as a result, the leggings were sort of twisted around their shins. Their uniforms had gathered much coal-dust grime from the trip upstream in the lighters. Their officers wore uniforms of similar cut and color, but of better grade cloth. As did the enlisted marines, they wore steel helmets. They were distinguishable by their leather boots and field Sam Browne belts and collar insignia. Most of them were of company grade. A lieutenant colonel was in over-all command of the landing. He knew exactly what he was doing. The operation reminded me of a circus's arrival, by wagon-load, at its show grounds. It seemed at first glance to be nothing but confusion compounded. But it wasn't that at all. It was a well-planned procedure, economically and beautifully executed. Even our critical officers began to be impressed.

We moseyed over to a detail which was putting the finishing touches on a howitzer nest. The corporal in charge looked us over in a rather startled way, then straightened up and saluted. "Good evening, sirs," he said. Digby Hand saluted him back. "Evening, Corporal," he said. "Nice job you're doing here. I'll speak to your colonel about it."

"Thank you, sir," said the marine.

We strolled along outside the barricade, sort of parading for the marines who had never seen or heard of a 15th infantryman before. Some saluted; some did not. It was all too much for Digby Hand. He addressed himself to a sergeant who was checking a heap of supplies: "All right, Marine, don't you know enough to salute an officer when you see one?" The sergeant gulped, stared at us, and brought up his hand to his tin hat. "Sorry, sir. I didn't see you. Too damn busy. It won't happen again, sir." "It better not," said Digby Hand.

For protection against what might happen when the marines found they had been saluting privates, we attached ourselves again to the rear of our group of officers. "You can't tell a marine a damned thing," one of the captains was saying. "They don't have to battle their way ashore here. All they have to do is land and march off. But no; each landing has to be bloodier than the rest. They bring along their own correspondents, you know. Pretty soon, the papers in the States will be full of stories how the marines against odds of one hundred to one captured Tientsin from the Chinese à la Boxer Rebellion days."

It grew darker; the marines installed acetylene lights to add to the illumination already provided by the Bund's lamps, and went on apace with their landing. A new flotilla of lighters brought up tanks and trucks and cannon. In trying to unload a tank—they were little tanks in those days, but they were heavy as lead—they broke the huge wooden boom on the edge of the Bund, the boom which the Chinese dock hands used to swing heavy stuff ashore. The marines cursed, found bridge timbers somewhere, bridged the lighter to the Bund's ramp, and simply drove their tanks and trucks ashore after that.

They had sent an advance detail to Tientsin before their landing, a group of officers charged with securing enough housing to accommodate four thousand men. This detail, working with some 15th Infantry officers, with the diplomatic corps, with Tientsin businessmen, and with Chinese civic officials, had leased yamens, godowns, compounds, hongs, hotels, and anything else empty, or which could be emptied hurriedly, that had a roof over it. The advance detail had also picked the spot on the Bund where the landings and unloadings would take place, and had mapped the routes through Tientsin's streets to the various sites where the men would be housed. They did a good job of it. Absolute order prevailed, and their time schedule was observed down to the minute. The officers, of course, knew there wasn't any war going on, but they were only too happy to practice a large-scale landing operation in a large, foreign city, and they went at it with gusto.

We were amazed at the amount of matériel the Fourth Brigade brought with it: tanks, field artillery, trucks, civilian-type automobiles, great heaps of military stores—and, to cap it all, twenty airplanes. We of the 15th Infantry had only mule-drawn forage wagons. Compared to Smedley Butler's marines, we were as a regiment out of the Civil War . . . brave with banners and muskets, and that was about all. In our barracks, we talked it over and became rather sullen about it. We, too, should have liked to have had modern trucks, tanks, artillery, and airplanes. Our officers were a bit miffed also. For one thing, Smedley Butler ranked Joseph Castner. That meant, if any shooting started, the 15th would have to fight under a marine. General Butler was world-famous. He had won the Congressional Medal of Honor during the fighting against the Boxers in 1900. He had garnered more honors in World War I. He had always believed in setting forth his views loudly, lucidly, and practically interminably.

As our officers had prophesied, the press in the United States gave adequate space to the marine landing in Tientsin. Some of the papers, indeed, even mentioned the fact that the 15th Infantry was already stationed in the city, and had been there for years. However, the marines were more colorful, there were a lot more of them, and they were the obvious saviors. Well, probably they were. At least, no war broke out.

Word filtered up to General Butler that his men were mistaking 15th Infantry enlisted men for officers and were saluting them on the streets, as the first arrivals had saluted Digby Hand, Martin Lord, and me down on the Bund. General Butler fulminated with more than usual intensity. He issued orders full of explication, denunciation, and commination. It got so that not even one of our majors could expect to be saluted when he encountered a marine on the street. Later, having calmed down somewhat, General Butler assessed the situation. As long as a 15th infantryman was dressed in his O.D. shirt, spiral puttees, and campaign hat, no one would or could mistake him for an officer. But once he put on his dress tunic with its gold buttons, his well-pressed slacks, his white shirt and black tie, his patent-leather-billed Pershing cap, it took a nice eye to discern that he was still a private. Well, General Butler argued, if a bunch of damned doughboys could look that snappy, so could his marines. He issued some more orders. The marines' battle tunics would be converted—overnight if possible—into the style of the tunics the 15th infantrymen wore; i.e., they would have roll collars, and the buttons on them would shine, shine, shine. Also, as rapidly as such wear could be brought over from the States, his men would be provided with the marine dress blues. Then he'd show the army a thing or two.

Seemingly every tailor in Tientsin was dragooned into the job of converting marine high-collar blouses into turn-down-collar affairs. The result was rather unhappy, because the high collars on the tunics didn't provide enough cloth for a decent roll collar, and what the tailor did achieve was always skimpy and, in many instances, downright silly-looking. There weren't any gold-plated marine buttons to be had in Tientsin, so the marines were ordered to scrape the black paint off their buttons and shine the metal. They did so, and produced buttons which looked like ancient, unwashed pennies. Our steel helmets were buffed and shellacked and bore shiny "Can-Do's" on them. The marines had to scrape the sanded camouflage off their helmets and buff and shellac them, and then drill holes in them and mount shined-up anchors and globes on them. They didn't like any part of it, but they did it.

Then there was the matter of our Springfield rifles. Fifteenth infantrymen, over the years, had boned and scraped and honed and rubbed linseed oil into the dress stocks of their Springfields until the wood of the rifles had become as beautiful as the finest ever turned out by the master gunmakers of France. But these were dress parade stocks. The stocks we used for drill and hikes and maneuvers and target shooting were the ordinary, untouched, sturdy walnut.

A Springfield is a Springfield, of course, the most accurate and probably the comeliest military shoulder weapon ever devised. But one clothed in a highly polished stock of beautifully grained wood is certainly a lot handsomer than one in a rough stock still oozing with cosmoline.

We of E Company were called out to form a guard for, and stand inspection by, General Smedley Butler the second day he was in Tientsin when he came to pay his respects to our General Castner. We lined up in the street outside the Compound wall in front of General Headquarters; and when Butler dismounted from his Cadillac with his aides we presented arms, and our captain gave him an extra snappy salute with his saber. (All infantry officers—and first sergeants—carried sabers in those days when they were on duty.) Butler saluted him back, looked him up and down, and said, "With your permission, Captain, I'd like to inspect your company." "It's a pleasure, sir," said our captain; and to us he snapped, "Order arms! Open ranks! Prepare for inspection!" He expected, and so did all of us, that General Butler would merely walk down the files and give a quick look. But when Butler inspected an honor guard, he inspected it. Digby Hand, being the tallest of us, was No. 1 in the front rank of the first squad. When Butler stopped in front of him, Digby snapped his rifle to inspection arms, flipping back the bolt and expecting Butler to pass on. He gave a definite jerk when the general swept the Springfield out of his hands, spun it, peered into the breech, peered down the barrel, and then practically threw it back at him. Smedley Butler that day wore his black dress uniform, gold braid, and snow-white gloves. When he was through inspecting our rifles, his gloves were still snow white. In Tientsin, the air was so dry that no oil was ever put on a gun; it might attract dust. We had been inspected by many officers before that, West Pointers mostly, who made a specialty of snap and precision in sweeping the rifle from the inspectee's hands, giving it a twirl and a jerk, noting the tiniest mote of dust on trigger guard or sight, or the least blur in its bore, then slamming it back to the soldier with an arm-breaking jar. But Smedley Butler had them all beat. We were very thankful—and so was our captain—that when he got through his gloves were still as white as when he had begun.

It was the stocks on our Springfields which fascinated him.

He held John Walsh's beautiful "guard-mount special" in his hands a moment or two, rubbed a gloved fingertip over the forearm, looked at John, and said, "Linseed?" "Yessir," said John, "and elbow grease." Our captain's hand tightened so on the haft of his saber that it looked as if his knuckles might burst, but he said nothing, and Butler said nothing. Butler did, however, give a little nod, as if he appreciated John Walsh's emendation.

And that very evening, every marine in the Fourth Brigade who toted a Springfield was put to work scraping the stock of his rifle with a bone and rubbing in linseed oil, with an added advisory of "not to spare the elbow grease." They were infuriated: What the hell was wrong with their Springfields the way they had been issued to them? They were weapons, not jewels. If the bores were clean and the bolts worked, what the hell else was neccessary? The company officers were inclined to go along with their men on that point, so a clarification seemed in order. It came promptly: General Butler had inspected a 15th Infantry honor guard and had been so impressed by the beauty of the guards' rifle stocks that he had decided the rifle stocks of his marines must be equally beautiful. Anything a soldier could do, a marine must do twice as well. This infuriated the leathernecks even more. They considered themselves as being strictly a rugged combat outfit, living under field conditions, raring to go. The idea of polishing and shining so as to compete in appearance with a sissified, understrength army regiment was abhorrent. But, by that time, the Fourth Brigade of Marines knew that when Smedley Butler issued an order he meant every word of it; and the price of linseed oil soared in Tientsin.

In a matter of a couple of weeks, the marines all had new roll-collar tunics with shiny buttons, and their steel helmets had been buffed and shellacked forest green. But the rifle stock business was ever to frustrate them. They had not the sixteen-year experience of the 15th Infantry behind them in such a matter, an experience which proved that every rifle had to have *two sets* of stocks, one scuffed and scarred and used for drill, the other boned and polished, wrapped lovingly in linseed-oily rags and used only for parade and guard mount. If Smedley Butler had ordered two sets of stocks for every Springfield rifle in his brigade, even his strongest admirers in the U. S. Marine Corps would have thought him a bit odd.

After the marines were well landed and housed and had become introduced—and thereby embittered—to the fact that for a long time they would have to compete with the 15th Infantry in dress, drill, and military snappiness, it became evident that there was never to be any love between the two organizations. Everywhere else they had landed in their long and illustrious career—the Halls of Montezuma, the Shores of Tripoli—they immediately had become the cocks of the walk because there had never been any military organization in being in those halls or on these shores which in any way could compare with them. In hall, on shore, only an enemy awaited, and the marines immediately set about fighting in order to get the job done.

But here in Tientsin, the complex, puzzling, and beautiful Chinese metropolis, there was such an organization in being, and it had been there for a long, long time. Indeed, it was a resident of Tientsin, as much a part of, and feature of, the city as Gordon Hall, or the Race Course, or the Yokohama Specie Bank. And it was in great part because of its residence that there was no fighting for the marines to do after they landed. There was nothing for them to do but shine and polish and drill and try to look as neat as the abominable soldiers who strolled in leisure around the yamens and the godowns, and watched the leathernecks at their toils. True, the leathernecks had tanks, they had trucks to haul their artillery pieces, they had twenty airplanes on a landing strip outside Tientsin; they were a potent fighting force, a precursor of the great combat teams which would appear in World War II; but here there was nothing for them to fight. When they emptied their latrines, when they did close-order drill on the streets, when they unloaded supplies from their lighters on the Hai Ho, there was always certain to be a sharply dressed soldier wearing "Can-Do's" standing there watching them. Oftentimes he was not even standing; he was sitting in a jinrikisha.

There was no love between them. At first there was some attempt at fraternization; we had them, in twos and threes, as our guests for dinner or supper; but our mess was so superior to theirs that, as had Bruce Ferguson of the Royal Scots, they made nuisances of themselves and wanted to eat with us all the time. Finally, an order had to be issued: no more inviting marines in for chow. There was no complementary order forbidding us to eat with the marines; it wasn't necessary. They had a general mess, cafeteria style, where you lined up with a mess kit and got it shoveled full of stew or beans. We had company mess on tables covered with tablecloths. We were served on china plates by mess coolies, and the meals we ate, in E Company at least when Anton Frerichs was mess sergeant, would have graced the cuisine of a French ocean liner.

The marines came in swarms to the little bars around our Compound, familiar, cozy little bars which had served 15th infantrymen for sixteen years, and which gave credit to good customers. We were uncouth and noisy enough, God knows, when we were at our drinking; but we were habituated—most of us were—to enjoying beer and gin fizzes and wine and vodka for their own sakes; we thought that fights spoiled evenings of quiet sipping. Not so the leather-necks. They were fresh out of the land of prohibition, and it seemed as if each one of them immediately set himself to the task of drinking China dry. It couldn't be done; too many 15th infantrymen had tried it in the past and failed.

The marines would boil into one of our little bars, usually in packs of a dozen strong, order everything in sight, whoop and holler and slop it down as fast as it was served, and then pick a quarrel either among themselves or with us. They inevitably started big arguments over the prices. Some of the bars were owned by dignified Chinese, some by White Russian women, some by Japanese, some by Europeans such as the old Swiss couple who ran the Café Genève. These owners welcomed the startling influx of trade at first; finally the day came when they talked about barricading their doors.

Our Military Police were few in number. Their main task was to stand post at the Compound gate, give directions to visitors, and examine parcels which the coolies might be carrying on leaving the American quarters. Two of them made the rounds of the bars late in the evening to warn the convivialists that bedcheck was near, but that was about all. Sometimes they had to arrest a drunken soldier; it happened once or twice a month. But the marines threw Military Police in platoon strength into the streets of Tientsin, literally because they had to. Most of these details roved about in the vicinity of our Compound. Other details were on constant duty in the bordello section of the French Concession. They had a full-time job. After all, four thousand men had landed.

Thus, where before we had been able to loaf at ease in peace and safety at the bars around our Compound, now there was no peace and very little safety any more. There were only hordes of marines trying to drink our bars dry, to fight us, or already fighting among themselves, with their Military Police swinging billy clubs and blowing whistles. "Good God," said little Calhoun Shaw, "I'd ruther the town was overrun with Mukden Lancers than like it is with these here animals."

It couldn't last, and it didn't. What brought it to a head was a fight at—of all places—an ice-cream parlor on Victoria Road. It was payday, and marines and 15th infantrymen were both in the place. Some insult over somebody's wife or girl friend was traded, and a fight flared up and flowed out into the street and seemed to engulf much of the downtown area. At any rate, it was entered by all the servicemen in the vicinity. Smedley Butler had the Call to Arms sounded; MPs from both commands herded the warriors back to their compounds. The story goes, and it is a good story, too good, probably, to be true, that General Butler, after his men were corraled, mounted a boxing ring in one of the marine compounds and said, "Men, you are to be commended for taking exception to an insult to one of our ladies, but your revenge has reached the stage where innocent persons are being injured. To assure that the conflict was brought to a halt, I have assembled you here where you will stay until the command goes out for training tomorrow morning. I will now take this matter up, in the proper way, with the army commander, to assure that there is no recurrence. *If there is, however,* I, myself, will lead you to clean up on the 15th Infantry."

There was no doubt in anyone's mind that he could have cleaned up. He commanded four thousand men, the army commander less than nine hundred.

Anyhow, a meeting of minds followed. The region around the 15th's Compound was placed off limits to the marines, and the off limits was enforced to the hilt. But that didn't mean that any off limits was set in retaliation against the 15th. Tientsin was our city, and we could still go where we chose. Grogshops and bordellos sprang up like weeds in the marines' immediate domain, and, as might be imagined, did a literally roaring trade. We saw not too much of the leathernecks after the demarcation line had been set for them. The streets around our own Compound had become peaceable again, and that was enough for us. It was now possible to walk down Victoria Road and not have to fight for one's life.

General Butler was always good news copy and was in excellent trim during this time in China. He held his first press conference in the U. S. Consulate and talked to all the American and foreign correspondents covering North China. The story goes—it may be apocryphal, but it sounds credible—that he said in effect, "We are here to protect foreign interests in China and are ready to fight to do it. If we have to fight, you may be sure that the streets will run with blood from gutter to gutter." The Consul General, Clarence Gauss, afterward Ambassador to China, is said to have had to call forth all his diplomatic ability—which was immense—to persuade the newshounds to agree to omit that portion of the general's talk.

In Tientsin that year no war developed, except the war between the marines and the 15th Infantry. It was only a tepid, athletic war fought on basketball courts, baseball diamonds, in boxing rings, and once on a football field. The marines won all the contests.

In the Peking-Tientsin-Shanhaikwan theater no war developed, either. Chiang Kai-shek, having rid himself of Communist ties and cut loose from Galen and Borodin, his Russian advisers, wooed the Young Marshal, Chang Hsueh-liang, to his side, along with the other leaders of the Northern Coalition. All affirmed their loyalty to Nanking, then Chiang's capital, and the sporadic war against the Chinese Communists opened. The Chinese Red armies then were mere hit-and-run peasant bands. Chiang's Nationalists gradually increased pressure upon them, pushing them hither and thither. In 1934-35, the Reds, under Mao Tse-tung, began their Long March to the Northwest, and in the wastes of Shensi Province established their stronghold. In 1936,

Chiang Kai-shek met Chang Hsueh-liang in rendezvous at Hsianfu. There, Chang kidnaped Chiang and held him until he agreed to end the civil war against the Communists and push instead the fight against the Japanese who were far advanced in their campaign to take over Manchuria. The day was rather late for that. The Japs had already set up their puppet, Henry Pu Yi, as the last Manchu emperor of China.

The war between Japan and Nationalist China formally started on July 7, 1937. Less than a year later, its position by then being untenable, the 15th U. S. Infantry was ordered home from Tientsin. The sparring between warlords, which the regiment had witnessed for a quarter of a century, was over. China's real agony had begun.

Chingwangtao

2 ✳

TENTING ON THE
OLD CAMPGROUND

1

In 1926, it was decided that the 15th Infantry needed
a formal summer camp, with permanent facilities and permanent rifle range, for use during the hot months when the
weather in Tientsin was all but unbearable. A site on the
Gulf of Pei Chih-li, three miles down the beach from the
city of Chingwangtao, was chosen. Chingwangtao is eighty
miles by rail from Tientsin, and twenty-five miles from
Shanhaikwan where the Great Wall of China begins. This
choice of a campsite was abetted by the Kailan Mining Administration, the then great British-Belgian-Chinese combine
which mined coal from Tongshan to the sea, owned its own
railway, its own collier fleet, its own police force, and was
almost an empire within its own right. Herbert Hoover, in
the days following the Boxer Rebellion, had helped lay out
and develop it. The pier at Chingwangtao was a particular
jewel in the KMA crown. It could accommodate deep-water

vessels. It was home port for KMA's colliers. It was the pier where the American transports docked, bringing 15th infantrymen to, and taking them away from, China. The KMA was only too happy at the idea of having a battalion of American soldiers almost within shouting distance of its pier all summer long when the warlords were most apt to do their fighting. (In the winter, the Gulf froze up, and so did the enterprise of the warlords.) Rights were gladly granted for the regiment to establish a camp on KMA ground among the sand dunes along the beach.

Before that, the regiment had had a sort of camp at Nan-Ta-Ssu, but the beach there did not compare with the beach at Chingwangtao, and other necessary conditions for an ideal summer camp were lacking. The move to the Chingwangtao site was welcomed by all.

A thirty-target rifle range was laid out, with firing lines at 200, 300, 500, 600, and 1000 yards. Auxiliary ranges were laid out for pistol fire, Stokes mortar and 27 mm. howitzer use; and a special range for the heavy Browning machine guns.

Company streets were laid out, with brick walks down the middle. Company mess halls were erected of wood. A flagpole was set up and, beside it, a wooden headquarters built. The Officers' Club, a beautiful thing of stone, was the center of Officers' Row, individual quarters of part wood, part canvas, part kaoliang matting. All the land was sand; at night the great moon of China would rise out of the Gulf and turn the Gulf, for a while, to gold.

To the north, you could see the Great Wall of China begin its fifteen-thousand-mile-long journey as it left the sea at Shanhaikwan like a tremendous snake and writhed off over the Jehol Mountains. The city of Chingwangtao was walled and off limits to 15th infantrymen. The Peking-Mukden Railway station at Chingwangtao was neat, trim,

clean as a pin. Nothing jarred. The little fishing villages along the Gulf fitted in. Martin Lord and I used to climb on the dunes sometimes in the evening and look around. It seemed strange that so much war—war through uncountable centuries—had been imposed upon such a pleasant land.

We enlisted men were housed under canvas in big army pyramidal tents, single-pole affairs with adjustable flaps at the peak and roll-up sides, the whole thing sitting on a wooden framework made of two-by-fours. We slept on army cots, and each cot had its mattress, its pillow, its sheets and pillowcase, and its mosquito bar. The company coolies made the beds up each morning and kept the tents tidy.

There was an orderly tent where the first sergeant did his paper work and where the company commander had his office. There was a supply tent where the supply sergeant and the company mechanic slept, and where the ammunition was stored. There was the barber tent with its two barber chairs where every morning the members of the company were shaved. An apprentice boy would lather up while the two barbers plied their razors. They could scrape the faces of the whole company in a very few minutes. Haircuts were given only in the afternoons.

There were four tents for our coolies, the No. 1 and No. 2 boys, the barbers, the mess coolies, and the squad coolies. As had been the custom in our Compound back in Tientsin, here in summer camp the mess coolies served us our meals and did the kitchen police, and the squad coolies shined our shoes, polished our buttons, kept our canteens full of cool water, and did the fatigue around the camp, such as bringing in supplies and sweeping the company street. All we did was eat and swim and shoot on the target range, and drink beer at night at Jawbone Charlie's *peng* back of the camp. We caught guard duty about once a week. Reveille was at four-thirty in the morning. Lights were out at night at 9 P.M. Camp activity usually stopped at noon. Almost every afternoon we took naps before going swimming.

Back in 1902, when the 15th had returned from the Philippines to Monterey, California, a young lieutenant by the name of Townsend Whelen was assigned to duty with the regiment. He had some definite ideas about rifle shooting, and he put them into practice with the 15th. He was one of the army's best rifle shots himself, and his counsel was heeded. The infantry weapon in those days was the .30-40 Krag, a five-shot bolt action magazine rifle which had replaced the single-shot .45 breech-loading Springfield, which in turn had supplanted the muzzle-loading .57 Springfield which the 15th had lugged in the Civil War. Now, this .30-40 Krag had long-range possibilities which had never been completely realized until Townsend Whelen began to exploit them. For one thing, the idea of hitting anything a thousand yards away had seemed ridiculous. But it didn't to Whelen. He argued it was just a matter of proper sight setting, proper wind allowance, and proper holding and squeezing. The Krag could do the rest. So forcefully did he impress his ideas on the 15th Infantry that the picked

squad which suffered under him at Monterey later walked off
with National Match honors at Sea Girt, New Jersey, and
shooting the thousand-yard range was no longer the figment
of an officer's dream.

Thus the 15th became, in Whelen's words, "quite a shooting regiment." It remained one, too, for in the loafing, lissome
days of the summers at Chingwangtao, just one thing
counted: rifle shooting. Colonel Isaac Newell, regimental
commander when I was with the 15th, was particularly
insistent upon it. "When an infantryman goes into battle,"
he said in one of his many exhortations on the subject,
"he carries with him his one means of offense and his one
means of defense. That is his Springfield rifle. Every infantryman's ability, in the last analysis, must be measured by
his ability with that weapon. If he can't hit anything, he is
not a good soldier. He is no good to himself, no good to
his comrades, no good to his officers. It would be better
for all concerned if he were just not there. But an infantryman who can be trusted to hit what he is told to hit when
he is told to hit it is a safeguard to himself, a bulwark
to his comrades, and a joy to his officers."

Camp regimen at Chingwangtao was relaxed. Fatigue
clothing was the prescribed dress, soft laundered blue or
brown denims, mix them or match them as you pleased.
You could wear a campaign hat, a fatigue hat, a garrison
cap, or no head covering at all. "Maskee the uniform," the
sergeants would say monotonously. *Maskee* is one of the
most wonderful words in any language. It means, roughly,
"just do as you please."

Reveille sounded at four-thirty in the morning. Each soldier had his own washbasin, and the company coolies would
bring steaming buckets of hot water to place on the wash
bench in front of the tents. The young men in their white
shorts sleepily piled out, washbasins in hand, along with
towel and toothbrush. The company street, theretofore

empty in the faint light of dawn, would suddenly become packed with tanned youths yawning over their ablutions. The barbers would be hopping about nervously, waiting for the rush upon their barber chairs. They had to shave the whole company before breakfast.

Breakfast was devoured even more prodigiously in summer camp than it had been back in Tientsin. Steak and eggs, ham and eggs, bacon and eggs, hot cakes and eggs, toast, marmalade; sometimes even fried chicken. And always great platters of cottage-fried potatoes and pitchers of coffee. We drank our coffee out of bowls, as the Chinese drank their tea. Then the details would form, some for the firing line, some for target pulling in the pits. The sun hardly would be up when we marched off. The men bound for the firing line would carry their Springfields, their cleaning rods, their shooting coats and score books, and bandolier after bandolier of ammunition. The pit details carried canteens of water and nothing else.

The pits were pits in name only. A wooden platform ran for some three hundred yards behind an eight-foot-high butt of masonry banked on the firing side with sand which had been sodded over. Safe behind that impenetrable butt, the pit details sat on benches and pulled the targets up and down and scored them and pasted up the bullet holes, and looked out onto the Gulf of Pei Chih-li. The targets were in frames like window frames, and ran up and down as do windows, the target in the rear counterbalancing the target in the front. The targets themselves were six-foot squares of heavy paper pasted on heavy burlap and mounted on frames of two-by-fours. They only lasted so long. The good shots drilled into the centers of them until the pasted stickers wouldn't hold any longer. The bad shots hit the wood of the frames and splintered it until it no longer could be shored up. Two men manned each target frame, shoving the target up and down together, and dividing the job of scoring and pasting up. The pit officer controlled everything with his whistle. Guards with red flags kept watch on the Gulf. When Chinese fishing boats drifted behind the pits, the whistle would blow and the red flags would wave; and down would come the targets, and there would be no more firing until the boats had drifted out of range.

It was pleasant work in the pits. We would first go to the range house and get the targets to be used that day, the bull's-eye targets for slow fire and the silhouette targets for rapid fire. We would carry them to the frames and mount them. The pit officer would check them and then phone to the firing line to say that everything was all set. Then, when things were similarly set on the firing line, the order would be given, "Targets up!" and, simultaneously over the top of the butt, thirty targets would pop up, each above its identifying numeral on the sodded embankment. On the line, the order would be given, "Commence firing!" and the Springfield rifles would begin to crack.

The .30-06 bullet leaves the muzzle of the viciously recoiling rifle with an ear-cracking blast and shrieks all the way down the range to the paper and burlap target. When it hits the target, it makes a loud whack! as if it had hit an animal, or perhaps a person. Sometimes a bad shot would strike the exposed masonry of the embankment, and the bullet would go ricocheting into the air. The screaming noise it made then is unspellable, but it sounds like a wounded banshee.

It was fun to sit there and watch the bullets blast into the targets. You couldn't see the actual bullet, of course, but you could see the holes pop. In slow fire, there was a long pause between pops. In rapid fire, the pops came rhythmically and speedily. You could always tell when an expert rifleman or sharpshooter was firing. His first shot might be out in the white, a foot or so away from the bull's-eye. You put a black spotter in the bullet hole, shoved the target up and scored the hit with an appropriate hand disc, and sat down and waited. There would be an interval while the rifleman back on the firing line—perhaps six hundred or a thousand yards away—consulted his score book and adjusted his sights. And then, whang! the next shot would be right in the black. In rapid fire, where the marking of the target was not done until the ten-shot string had been completed, you could tell the expert or the sharpshooter by the way he was grouping his shots. A really good marksman would bunch his shots in an area small enough to be covered by a campaign hat. The bum shot would scatter his so much that a spread-out pup tent couldn't cover them.

Once, when Wild Bill Tuttle was pit officer he was standing by Martin Lord and me, watching the shooting. It was rapid fire at five hundred yards. There, the rifleman shot from the prone position and had sixty seconds to get off his string of ten. He began firing with one five-shot clip of bullets in his magazine, and had to reload with a second clip when the first was exhausted. He couldn't argue about the time his target was exposed, because it went up at the pit officer's signal and came down, after sixty seconds, again at the pit officer's signal. The flag at the pits was waved vigorously for three seconds before the target shot up, and that was all the warning the riflemen on the line was given.

We never knew who it was who was shooting at our target from five hundred yards back that morning. But his first five shots made a beautifully tight group in the center but just under the black of the silhouette. Each shot could only score a four. Wild Bill looked at the target critically as the bullets tore into it. "He's got his sights set a fraction too low," said Wild Bill. "When he puts in a new clip, ease the frame down about five inches, and let's let him make a few bull's-eyes." So, in the miniscule interval in which it took the rifleman to reload, we inched his target down a little. This was not perceptible at the firing line, of course.

But his next five shots went spang! spang! spang! into the black. "Colonel Newell would court-martial me if he knew I did anything like that," said Wild Bill amiably, and walked on.

Along about eight-thirty in the morning, the coolies would bring us out baskets of chow from the company mess hall, and everybody on the range and in the pits would take a lunch break. We were usually half-starved by then, because we had eaten breakfast at five; and we would tear into whatever the coolies brought with wolflike rapacity. Some of the company mess sergeants took advantage of that morning lunch period to get rid of their leftovers, knowing the men would eat anything put in front of them. Thus, in some extreme cases when their company mess fund happened to be low, the men might get sandwiches made of two pieces of bread with a leaf of cabbage mayonnaised between them. The complaining howls which would arise were heart-rending, but the sandwiches would disappear. In E Company, however, this never happened. Our mess sergeants, Frerichs first, and Gatowka, his replacement, were foreign-born men, Frerichs from Germany and Gatowka from Finland. They came from farming communities where one rose before dawn to go into the fields, and where one usually ate five times a day. Both thoroughly approved of the morning lunch, even though it meant extra work for them. Frerichs thought it ought to be rather fancy: doughnuts, pie, cake, tarts, and the like. Gatowka thought it ought to be more solid; heaps of fried fish and buttered bread was his specialty. Both considered tea the ideal morning drink, black tea, smoking hot, unsugared. At eighty-thirty or nine o'clock, the whistle would blow, and we in the pits would rush down to the beach to wash our pasty hands in the water of the Gulf, and then race back for big helpings of Frerichs' cake and tarts or Gatowka's fish and a canteen cup full of scalding tea.

Once some sailors from the cruiser U.S.S. *Marblehead*, the "Swayback Maru" of World War II fame, were sharing the pits with us. The *Marblehead* had tied up at the KMA pier, and her captain had decided to give his tars some much needed rifle practice. They came ashore on the beach below our camp in their beautiful launches, and we turned the target range over to them for a couple of days until the ship's whole complement should have a chance to shoot. We stood by them in the pits to show them how to operate the targets, and we stood by them on the firing line to coach them in the use of the Springfield. As usual, at eight-thirty in the morning, our mess coolies brought out the baskets of lunch. Gatowka was mess sergeant then, and the lunch was fried fish and corn bread. The fish had been taken from the sea only an hour or two before by the Chinese fishermen who daily seined in the Gulf. Back in the mess hall, Gatowka had grumbled to himself, "Dem damn sailors got to eat, too, I guess," and he sent along extra baskets of loaves and fishes. Our coolies went down the line, offering the food to soldier and sailor alike. "What the hell?" asked the surprised petty officer, who was sitting with Digby Hand and me. "Usual morning snack," explained Digby. "Grab some and stow it away. It's here to eat and not jest to set and look at."

"Snack?" said the petty officer. "And you mean they pack it out to you?"

"Well, chief, you see 'em, don't you?" said Digby. "Things is different in the army from what they is on the high seas. You see, they work us so hard here in the 15th thet they gotta feed us extra to keep up our strength."

"Work, hell," said the petty officer. "All I ever seen yuh do is jest lay around and eat and get waited on."

"We signed up for soldiering, and soldiering is all we do," said Digby. "We got a guy that manicures our toenails, too, you know."

"I don't doubt it, fella. I reckon you also got a guy to brush yer teeth."

"We're working on it, chief. We're working on it."

That afternoon, on the firing line, the petty officer watched as Digby Hand, illustrating at the navy's behest a fine point or two in offhand shooting, stood up at his six-feet-two, snuggled the rifle's sling strap tightly around his left arm, tucked the rifle butt into his right shoulder, parted his feet, brought the rifle down to level, froze into supple rigidity, and proceeded to make five bull's-eyes at two hundred yards as fast as he could work the bolt. "It's thet extra food we get that does it," explained Digby to the petty officer, who had experienced great difficulty in just hitting around the edges of the target, much less making any bull's-eyes. "It's thet extra food and beer at night."

"And don't forget the laying around and getting waited on hand and foot," sneered the sailor.

"I don't never forget it," said Digby. "I'd be taking a three-hour siesta this here very afternoon if I didn't hafta be out here showing you mud ducks how to shoot."

Summer camp at Chingwangtao ended in late September, and back to Tientsin went the battalion. Left to guard the camp through the long Siberian-like winter was a detachment of twenty-one privates, a sergeant, three corporals, and a lieutenant. Two of the mess halls were winter-proofed with tar paper and converted into barracks, army cots and foot lockers replacing the mess tables. Big coal-burning heating stoves were set up. Fur caps, sheepskin coats, and felt overshoes were issued. Everything was snugged down and boarded up so that the men could guard the camp and its equipment and supplies with a minimum of surveillance. The lieutenant lived in a stone cottage off Officers' Row, occupied during the summer by the commanding officer. It was an architectural marvel with an inside toilet, bathtub, fireplace, and everything.

Before the autumn freeze came and the snow fell, there was a period of light, persistent rain; and it was then that migratory water fowl visited the region in incredible numbers. General Castner, whose chief hobby besides long marches was hunting, bethought himself of this one boring fall day in his Headquarters office in Tientsin, and he wondered if the birds had begun to arrive in the marshes beyond the camp at Chingwangtao.

One of his aides was ordered to check with the companies to ascertain if any of the men from the camp's winter guard detail happened to be in the Compound. Yes, in E Company, we had one, Private Zorgaleski, who had come up to get a tooth pulled and who was to leave on the night train.

The aide found Zorgaleski, told him to get in proper uniform, and report to the general on the waterfowl situation. "Gosh, sir," said Zorgaleski, "I ain't been hunting or nothing. We been awful busy nailing things up, and then we generally play chess or something. I don't know nothing to say."

"Well, think of something damned quick and get over and tell it to the general," snapped the aide, and left.

Zorgy slowly got into his dress uniform, his hands trembling. "I don't know nothing about no damn birds," he kept saying.

Martin Lord took pity on him. "Look, kid; it's simple. Tell the general the snow geese are flying, and that there's a lot of brant mixed in with them. Tell him that the stretch of checkerboard woods east of camp is lousy with woodcock. Tell him that the jack curlew are in the river marsh, and so are the scaup ducks. Tell him stuff like that; that's what he wants to hear."

"Yeah, but gosh, Martin, suppose he goes down there and don't see nothing like that? He'd likely have me shot."

"Aw, there's bound to be a few ducks. There always are. If there aren't any brant or curlew, you can tell him they flew on."

"But I don't know a brant from a road-runner."

"Of course you don't, but the general does."

A call came up from the orderly room: "Zorgaleski, report to the commanding general at once."

"Jeez," said Zorgy, "write them bird names down fast for me, will you, Martin?"

Lord did so. "Just tell the general you jotted this down after the aide told you what was wanted."

"You reckon he'll believe me?"

"Of course he'll believe you. You've got an awful trustworthy face. Now race on over there and mind your manners."

Zorgaleski went and, after half an hour, returned.

"Well, how'd it go?" asked Martin.

"Aw right, I guess."

"What do you mean—all right?"

"Well, the general's going down to camp tonight on the same train as me, and he wants me to guide him when we get there. That woodcock stuff you wrote down really set him afire."

"Ummm," said Lord. "That's what happens when you let your enthusiasm get the upper hand. Best of luck, Zorgy. Now you're gunbearer to the general."

"I druther not be, by God."

After he left, I said, "Look, Martin, why the hell did you get him to tell the general there's woodcock down there? You never saw a woodcock in your life, and you know it."

"I never saw a brant or a scaup duck either," said Lord. "But where there's woods, there's bound to be woodcock. In this case, there'd better be. I'll say a little prayer for Zorgy tonight."

In about a week, our company commander got a communiqué from the general's office. Martin Lord saw it when he was acting as charge-of-quarters and had a chance to squint through the captain's correspondence in the late hours of the night after everybody else had gone to bed.

The communiqué said: "The Commanding General directs me to inform you that he deems Private Oleg Zorgaleski to be *First-Class Private* caliber, and he directs that he be so promoted at once. The General was agreeably pleased with Private Zorgaleski's military appearance and with his keen powers of observation, especially where migratory fowl are concerned. The General expects that *First-Class Private* Zorgaleski will be available for guide duty when the General makes his next hunting trip to the 15th Infantry's camp at Chingwangtao."

"Those woods must have been really full of woodcock," said Martin Lord.

THE NIGHT CRAWLER

2 ❋

Early one morning in July of 1927, the four soldiers who slept in the tent ahead of the one I slept in awoke and found their shoes missing. They thought it some sort of joke, but they didn't laugh. First, they angrily blamed each other; then, agreeing that the occupant of some other tent was to blame, they decided upon an immediate tent-by-tent shakedown.

Presently, the delicious early morning languor of the tent I was in was shattered as our four neighbors stormed in and began pawing into our barracks bags, tossing our things around, and peering under our cots. They were bronzed, muscular youths, clad only in their shorts. "What's the idea?" Martin Lord demanded. "Somebody swiped our shoes," one of the visitors snarled. "When we find him, we're going to chop off his head." And they stormed into the next tent. In a matter of minutes, they had all of E Company in an uproar.

Down the company street, we could hear the cursing and screaming of other affronted tent dwellers. Martin Lord, Digby Hand, little Calhoun Shaw, and I peered out of our tent to see what was happening. Fist fights were breaking out. All this was quite unprecedented, for summer camp was usually little short of idyllic. The members of E Company had expected to rise in their customary fashion, shower in fresh, cool water, be shaved by the company's barbers, eat an enormous breakfast of steak and eggs, and then go out to the target range and shoot the Chief of Infantry's Course. Afterward, the soldiers would hurry to the beach and bathe in the limpid waters of the Gulf; on returning to camp they would down an enormous dinner of fried chicken, and then take a siesta, and finally, in the evening, they would stroll over to Jawbone Charlie's *peng* for a round or two of lovely German beer.

That morning, however, the situation soon became so bad that the first sergeant, a lean tough man named Turner, was forced to take notice. He wore six hash marks on the sleeve of his blouse, plus two wound stripes he had gained in World War I. Striding down the company street, he shouted in bitter tones those selfsame words which first sergeants have used throughout the history of military organizations, "What in the name of hell is going on around here?" It took much explanation, for everyone was badly confused by that time, to make clear to Turner the fact that four pairs of shoes were missing. "All right," said Turner, "Everbody back to your tents—except you, you, you, and you," and he singled out four men at random. "Now then, we will make a physical check on every pair of shoes in this company, and when we get to the bottom of it I'm gonna kill the guy that swiped 'em."

We returned to our tents. Turner and his checkers came

along like a hurricane and heaved every shoe within the tents out into the company street. Then Turner made every man in the company pick his own shoes out of the scattered heaps. Each of us had a clothing number, and this number was stamped on the underside of the tongues of our shoes, so the identification was not too hard to accomplish. But all it proved was that there were twelve pairs of shoes missing instead of only four.

"Straighten out your tents and go get your breakfast," said Turner, wiping his face with one sleeve. "I'll have to take this up with the company commander."

The officer in command of E Company was a West Pointer, a very able first lieutenant whom the men had nicknamed Felix the Cat. (He was one of many 15th Infantry officers who were to become generals in World War II.) While the company was eating its breakfast and gabbling over the mystery, Felix the Cat and Turner sat down in the office tent and surveyed the situation. Either a soldier had stolen the shoes, they reasoned, or one of the camp coolies had stolen them, or some outside Chinese had done it. That left the field wide open. Felix the Cat and Turner decided that a soldier was the most likely culprit. It was eight days till payday, and some thirsty private, or even some noncommissioned officer, might have taken the shoes with the idea of surreptitiously trading them to Jawbone Charlie for beer. Indeed, he might have done this the night before, because no one knew the exact hour the shoes were taken.

So, even before breakfast was finished, First Sergeant Turner came into our mess hall and, again picking at random, ordered three other soldiers and me out for duty. Our mission was to accompany Felix the Cat to Jawbone Charlie's *peng*, and search it for shoes. Charlie's *peng*, a shed made of matting and poles and furnished with tables and benches, stood well behind the camp. Back of the *peng* was a storage lean-to in which Charlie stacked up his beer cases and iced the bottles. In the lean-to also was a pallet he slept on.

"I no trade beer for shoes," said Charlie indignantly when Felix the Cat accosted him. "You look-see."

"Just what we intend to do," said Felix the Cat. Then he noticed a sand-and-matting-covered mound behind the lean-to. "What's that?" he demanded.

"Is ice," said Charlie. He walked over and, lifting up a piece of matting, disclosed what looked like hunks of mud. "Ice, see," he said. Ice in that part of North China was cut from ponds in the winter and stored in big piles covered with layers of sand and straw and matting. Given enough ice to begin with, the piles would last throughout the summer. As the summer wore on, the ice would become muddier and muddier.

There was nothing else to search at the *peng*, so Felix the Cat gave up. However, he warned Charlie that any trading of beer for shoes or any other negotiable army commodity would mean the end of Charlie's beer business as far as the camp was concerned. Charlie nodded his head gravely in agreement. Then he led us back to a table, and, setting out five bottles of nicely chilled Spatenbräu, he said, "On the house." It was the first time in our lives the other soldiers and myself had ever drunk beer with a commissioned officer.

Felix the Cat wasn't the man to let the loss of a dozen pairs of shoes reduce his company's efficiency or interfere with its training program. Later that morning, he wired regimental headquarters in Tientsin to send down more shoes. Then he made those of us who had extra shoes share them with those who had lost theirs, and, only two hours behind schedule, marched the company out to the rifle range where, in individual squads, we shot the Chief of Infantry's Course.

We didn't get any siesta that afternoon, however. To discipline us for losing the shoes, Felix the Cat decreed that we put on our Hong Kong khaki dress uniforms after dinner and that our non-coms give us close order drill for two hours. We did squads right, right by squads, etc., in the loose sand, while the rest of the battalion, attempting to snooze in the coolness of their tents, objected violently but futilely to the irate bellowings of our corporals.

There wasn't any going to Jawbone Charlie's that night, either. Felix the Cat decided the thief might return; he stationed a guard at each end of the company street, and he ordered the rest of us to stay in our tents until Reveille the next morning. The skirts of our tents were tied up to the low eaves to allow the air to enter. When we went to bed, we always put our shoes under our cots. Things began very dully that night. We played cards by candlelight or simply lay on our cots and shot the bull. One by one, we dropped off to sleep. An hour or two after Taps, a shot rang out, followed by cries that sounded as if they came from the depths of hell. Company E, en masse, poured out of its tents—fifty-six young men in white shorts, some clutching their Springfields. It was all very unmilitary, but Sergeant Turner soon corrected this. At his command, we fell in and stood at attention.

Felix the Cat came on the double from Officers' Row. After about half an hour, we found out what had happened. A sentry at one end of the company street had seen something sneaking along in the darkness. He had challenged it, and, when he received no answer, fired. He had hit a dog, one of those huge North China mongrels we called gravediggers, because of their fondness for digging into fresh graves. The .30-06 Springfield bullet had ripped through the dog's lungs, and the animal's dying protests were what had sounded like wails from hell.

Felix the Cat complimented the sentry. "Good work," he said. "That's what you were posted here for. That gravedigger didn't steal the shoes, but after seeing what has happened to it the real thief will think twice before prowling around this company again. Send out a dog-burying detail, Sergeant. The rest of you men get back to your tents and stay there. We have alert sentries on the job tonight."

At Reveille the next morning, a new group of soldiers— twelve of them—awoke and found their shoes missing. Felix the Cat got himself under control in about fifteen or twenty minutes. "It's pretty clear now, isn't it?" he said to Sergeant Turner, after we had all lined up in the company street. "While we were fooling around with that dog, our friend sneaks down the back row and helps himself to more shoes. When I think of the milling mob E Company made of itself after that shot was fired, I could almost turn in my bars."

Marching out to the target range that morning, some of the men were without shoes, for we were running out of spares. These shoeless ones groused at first, but later on decided that going barefoot was fun; the warm sand felt good to their feet. The companies we passed on the way to the range knew about our lack of footwear and guyed us considerably. "Coxey's Army" was a favorite barb.

The air was very clear that day, and, looking north, one could see the Great Wall of China twenty-five miles away. Much closer to view was the Kailan Mining Administration pier, jutting out into the Gulf from the city of Chingwangtao. The air was loud with a mournful chanting. This came from a band of fishermen, hauling in their nets along the beach, about a mile from the target range. The fishermen took their nets out twice a day, once in the late morning and again after midnight, and their chanting was a plea to the Sea God to fill their nets.

The chanting must have impinged somehow on Felix the Cat's consciousness. About one o'clock in the afternoon, just when we were beginning our siesta, he decided, apparently, that the fishermen were probably the ones who were stealing our shoes. The fisherfolk lived in a huddle of little matted huts at the water's edge, far down from the target range, and they were, Felix the Cat must have thought, so wretchedly poor that they would steal anything. At any rate, he decided to raid the village.

He also decided to make the raid as impressive as possible —a kid-glove, fancy-dress affair. He selected the squad I was in and ordered us to garb ourselves as if we were about to mount formal guard. That meant Hong Kong khaki pressed until creases were razor sharp, buttons and collar ornaments polished until they sparkled like jewels, and cap visors and shoes shined until they glowed like rare metal. But no guns, because we didn't want to risk provoking the Chinese authorities. Guns were out. We would cow the villagers by the bravery of our uniforms.

Felix the Cat dressed himself in his own immaculate khaki, gleaming boots, and gleaming Sam Browne belt, and summoned Big Jim, E Company's No. 1 boy, to come along as interpreter. Big Jim was about fifty years old, and weighed about two hundred pounds. He wore a blue gown, black skullcap, and army shoes. The other company coolies all had to pay squeeze to Big Jim to hold their jobs. In addition to English, Big Jim spoke Russian and German, having learned the former from the Russians living in Tientsin and the latter from the German troops when they were stationed in the city after the Boxer Rebellion and for whom Big Jim had once worked.

The day was warm and beautiful, and like a drill team we swung at a hundred and twenty-eight steps a minute down the moist, firm sand of the beach road toward the fishing village. It was the same road on which, centuries before, the hordes of the great khans, Kublai and Genghis, had thundered down out of Manchuria. On our arrival, and on signal from Felix the Cat, our corporal barked out an extra-military "Squad, halt! Stand at ease!"

Said Big Jim to Felix the Cat, "These very ignorant people, sir Lieutenant. They no savvy this stuff."

The fisherfolk were peering at us from their huts. The men wore white pajamalike pants; their heads were shaven. The women wore blue pajamalike things. The children wore nothing. All that weren't barefoot wore slippers. There were about fifty or sixty persons in the village.

"Tell these people that we have come as representatives of the American camp to say hello and look around a little," Felix the Cat said to Big Jim.

The villagers were nervous. "They very stupid, sir Lieutenant," Big Jim said. "They no savvy stuff like that."

"Tell 'em anyhow, dammit!" snapped Felix the Cat.

So Big Jim yammered at the fisherfolk, and the fisherfolk yammered back, and finally Big Jim said, "They say, sir Lieutenant, American bullet almost hit boat when they out today fishing."

"Tell them to keep their boats away from in back of the target range," said the lieutenant. "They ought to know better, anyway."

More yammering. "They say you shoot dog. Very bad," said Big Jim.

"Tell them," said Felix the Cat, "I'll shoot all their dogs if they don't keep them out of our camp."

"They say dog very valuable," said Big Jim, after more parleying. "These people talk very bad Chinese, sir Lieutenant. Very hard understand."

"You're doing all right," said Felix the Cat. "How did we get sidetracked on that fool dog, anyhow? What's cooking in that big pot? It stinks to heaven."

Big Jim, amid the protests of the fisherfolk, went over and peered into an iron pot that stood on a bed of coals close by.

"This the dog, sir Lieutenant," he said. He turned and spoke to the fisherfolk, and they replied to him sharply.

"They dig him up after you shoot him. They like better than fish. So now they cook. They fix big dinner. Everybody eat. But they afraid now you come to eat the dog."

"Tell them that nothing is farther from our intentions. Tell them also that I think they stole our shoes as well as dug up the dog. Tell them I'm going to search their huts."

Big Jim told them, and the yammering rose to a shriek. The head fisherman spat at Felix the Cat. "He say his house his house. He no let you look-see," explained Big Jim.

"Tell him to try and stop me," the lieutenant said. "Come on, you men. Keep them away while I have a look."

So, embarrassedly, we stationed ourselves like the defensive line of a football team before the entrance of the main hut, and Felix the Cat gingerly went in under the greasy burlap that served as a door. We kept the angry fishermen away by shaking our fists at them. Felix the Cat searched the huts one after another as the fisherfolk howled and yelled. He had soon had enough. "Nothing in them but rags," he said. "Just piles of stinking rags. The dog's hide is in the big one. It's the worst smelling of all. I wonder why in hell I put in for China duty. Fall in. Let's go."

That night, eight pairs of shoes were stolen from H Company, the machine-gun outfit, which was bivouacked at the far end of the camp. Seven O.D. shirts were also missing. Next morning, the temporary battalion commander, a captain acting for the major who was away somewhere, decided it was time to step in and take over. As a shavetail, he had earned the name of Scatterbrain. He assembled the battalion in a half-circle about him and told it his views. He said, "Men—or perhaps I should say children—somebody, or some group of bodies, has robbed this camp of thirty-two pairs of shoes and seven shirts and God knows what else. This will stop at once. It will stop even if it becomes necessary for every damned one of you to wear your shoes twenty-four hours a day on your feet and tie your remaining shoes around your fool necks. I do not intend to end my career in the army as the battalion commander who let his shoes get stolen. The company commanders have been informed of the orders I have caused to be issued. I used to think this was a pretty good outfit, I used to be kind of proud of it, but now I guess you need nursemaids and amahs to carry you through. This condition will change. As of now. Company commanders, dismiss your troops."

Felix the Cat marched E Company back to its tents. There he formed us in a half-circle about *him*, and he added his endorsement to what Scatterbrain had said. Felix the Cat spoke more in sorrow than in anger. He said a blot on the company's record was a blot on his own record, and after playing on that theme for a while he relayed to us the battalion commander's orders. In addition to the guards in the company streets at night, there would be two sentinels posted behind the tents of each company. In addition to that, the men in the squad tents would take turns staying on watch within the tents all night. All shoes, shirts, and other articles of clothing that formerly had been shoved under cots at night or strewed on tent floors would be stowed away in barracks bags and the bags tied securely to the tent poles. The non-coms would enforce these orders. There would also be special guards posted at the mess halls, supply tents, and office tents. We were to become an armed camp. We wouldn't get much sleep, but neither would we lose any more shoes. All this extra security, Felix the Cat went on, was to be carried out in utmost secrecy. The battalion commander wanted the camp to look its usual sloppy, careless self at night. He wanted the thief to think all was safe for another incursion. He wanted, in short, to trap the thief— and, if any man gave away that trap, woe betide him.

The first night under the new security measures, nothing at all happened. And there were no shoes or shirts missing in the morning. It was the same the second night. The third night, another gravedigger elected to do some prowling around the camp. Everything repeated itself. A G Company sentinel saw it, shot at it, and wounded it. In its pain, the dog went screaming and skittering among the tents. Soldiers poured out into the company streets. Non-coms yelled "Hold your fire!" Officers poured down from Officers' Row. A machine-gun-company sentinel killed the gravedigger with two quick shots from his automatic pistol. In the morning, G Company reported three pairs of shoes missing.

Scatterbrain restricted G Company to its quarters. The men who had lost their shoes had, it seemed, disobeyed his orders about putting the shoes in barracks bags and tying the bags to tent poles. The company non-coms had disobeyed his orders in not seeing to it that the men had done so. What Scatterbrain said to the company commissioned officers was kept private. There were rumors that the regimental commander was coming down from Tientsin to take personal charge.

That same day, Scatterbrain issued a new order: Anyone who shot another gravedigger would be court-martialed. The basis of this order was the growing belief that the thief had deliberately brought the dog to camp and then, in the comparative safety of the hell that broke loose when some sentry shot a dog, had done his looting unnoticed. Scatterbrain attached this addendum to his order: "The appearance of a Chinese mongrel dog, commonly called gravedigger, in this camp at night will mean that the thief is about to strike again. Sentinels and guards, on noting the appearance of such a beast, will withhold their fire, but will give the QUIET ALARM and redouble their vigilance."

For a few nights, nothing happened. The tension finally eased so much that the soldiers in their tents would bark and growl, gravediggerlike, at the sentries who paced up and down the company streets. Then one night, when I had sentry duty on the midnight to 2 A.M. shift, I saw something moving on the ground behind the tents. It was one of those nights when the moonlight, filtering through the clouds, softly illumines the earth. The fishermen, as usual, were chanting mournfully out in the Gulf. The thing I saw looked vaguely like a lumpy crocodile worming along through the sand under some thornbushes. I decided it must be a dog. But it wasn't a dog, for presently a real dog—a huge grave-digger—trotted up, halted, smelled at the thing, then shied away sharply and bounded off into the sand wastes. Because I didn't know what else to do, I gave the QUIET ALARM— two soft bleats on my whistle. At the bleats, the thing in the thorn scrub moved snakewise around and seemed to stare at me. "Corporal of the guard!" I yelled.

The corporal's guard, already on their feet because of the QUIET ALARM, sprinted down the company street, and the thing stood up and tried to take off into the thorn scrub. But one of its feet hit a tent peg driven into the sand and partly drifted over, and the thing tripped and fell full length and let out little mews of dismay.

Out of the dark plunged Felix the Cat, who had been checking on his sentries, and he flung himself on the thing. The corporal's guard and I gathered around in a circle, flashlights glaring, and Felix the Cat got to his feet and lifted up what he had captured.

It was a Chinaman, a pigtailed Chinaman—small, young, and with a shockingly pock-marked face. He was completely naked. He had coated his body with grease and then had rolled in the sand until he looked like a man made out of sand. Two burlap sacks, also greased and smeared with sand, were tied around his neck and hanging down his back. In one of them were two pairs of shoes. He stood there very docilely under the muzzles of our guns.

Felix the Cat brushed at himself in a futile attempt to cleanse his uniform of the greasy sand that befouled it.

After some cogitation, he ordered the prisoner placed in the guard tent with two sentries for the rest of the night.

I helped guard the prisoner the next morning, when the battalion officers convened and held a hearing. He was a nice little chap. We gave him a pan of water and soap and towels, and he scrubbed himself clean of his grease and sand. We also gave him some old fatigues to wear, and he looked very neat in them and somehow girlish after he had rebraided his pigtail. He ate a mammoth breakfast of soft-boiled eggs, ham, and toast, and drank a full quart of hot coffee. We asked him his name, but nobody could make out his answer —even Big Jim—so for the record he was listed as Chang Doe, a pun proudly thought up by Felix the Cat, because in North China, *Chang* is pronounced *Johng*.

The 15th Infantry held, or at least claimed, quasi-magisterial powers over the Chinese who worked for the regiment; hence, by extension, the battalion officers argued that the same powers applied in Chang Doe's case. His crime was a military matter and not one for Chinese civil authority, which was vague anyhow.

Chang Doe, happy in his new clothes and stuffed to bursting with his breakfast, laughed and giggled and answered yes to everything the officers asked. Big Jim was interpreter.

Had he stolen all the shoes?

Giggle. Yes.

How many shoes had he stolen?

Giggle, giggle. Many times more than the fingers on both his hands.

Here Big Jim said, "Gentlemen officers sirs, this man not right in head. Too much giggle."

"Never mind the comments, Jim," said Felix the Cat. "Just interpret. Ask him if he used dogs to help him when he raided the camp."

Big Jim spoke to Chang Doe, who howled with laughter. "He say," said Big Jim, "dog very good to eat. He happy when you shoot. He crazy, gentlemen officers sirs, like I say before."

"Ask him where the shoes are," said Felix the Cat.

Big Jim put the question. Chang Doe giggled. "He hide them by his father's house," said Big Jim.

Here the battalion commander took over. "Draw up a detail of men, Lieutenant," he said to Felix the Cat. "We will go at once to this man's father's house and get those shoes."

So a platoon of us formed, and Chang Doe led us to his father's house. It was away from the sea, away from the camp and the target range, deep in the artificial forest planted by the Kailan Mining Administration alongside its railroad tracks. The trees were planted in crisscross straight rows, and the forest was the "checkerboard" where First Class Private Zorgaleski had led General Castner on the successful woodcock hunt. Chang Doe's father's house was a tiny hut made of twigs and mud and mats and sticks. In front of the house, on a stool, sat Chang Doe's father. He was the image of his son, except for a wispy white beard. At a little fire he was roasting some peanuts for his meal.

The father smiled and bowed to us, then wept when Big Jim told him what we were doing there. Before we could stop him, he picked up a stick and beat Chang Doe over the head with it. Chang Doe began to weep also. "Old father say bad son has disgraced him," Big Jim said. "He ask if you like peanuts. He cook some for you. He not knowing anything about shoes."

Felix the Cat declined the peanuts and demanded to be led immediately to the shoes. Chang Doe took us out of the forest to a concrete culvert under the KMA tracks. There he had built himself a series of mud shelves. And there on the shelves were the shoes, neatly arranged according to size. All the shoes were very shiny. A shoeshine kit, obviously stolen by Chang Doe on one of his forays, stood on one of the shelves. The shirts were there, too, carefully folded on a separate shelf.

"He very silly in head," said Big Jim. "He play store. But his father not knowing about it."

By a military court assembled the next day Chang Doe was tried for stealing military equipment and sentenced to thirty days' hard labor in and about the Second Battalion's summer camp. That meant three soldiers had to take turns standing watch on him while he slept all through the night in the guard tent. A sentry had to follow him around all day with rifle and bayonet as he went about with broom or shovel tidying things up. The sergeant of the guard had to think up other things for him to do. As I said, the prisoner was a nice little guy, and we all grew very fond of him. He preferred shining shoes to anything else, and always shined his guard's shoes at least twice a day. His father was allowed to visit with him every evening at mealtime and to share supper with him.

Father and son both wanted to come along with us when we broke camp to return to Tientsin, but Felix the Cat said no. It was a rather emotional leave-taking. We gave Chang Doe and his father a pair of old army shoes and an old O.D. shirt apiece, and we also gave Chang Doe a new shoeshine kit. Father and son wept as we left.

THE GREAT WALL
OF CHINA

3

What had started out one summer in the camp at Chingwangtao potentially to be a platoon-strength expedition soon narrowed itself down to a five-man enterprise. Its mission was to see what the Great Wall of China looked like from the other side. It was the chaplain's idea. He had contemplated the way we spent our idle hours, loafing around on our bunks, lying on the beach, guzzling beer, or just dreaming. It seemed silly to him for young men to waste *all* their time that way.

So, in order to vary the monotony of our lives, he proposed to organize some sight-seeing tours. The place of all places to sight-see was obviously the Great Wall. It began at the city of Shanhaikwan and went rolling off over the Jehol Mountains. The Peking-Mukden Railway connected

Shanhaikwan with Chingwangtao, so transportation was simple enough. The chaplain thought that any young man would be delighted to make the trip. He took his idea up with our company commander, saying he would like to canvass the members of the company with the idea of forming an expedition . . . an expedition which he hoped would be so successful that it would set the pattern for other such tours in the future. "You can ask them," said our captain.

The chaplain put it to us one day when we came trooping back from a swim in the Gulf. "Hold it, hold it," he said, halting us with outstretched arms. He pointed at the Wall: a purple line on a mountain. "There it is," he said, "the Great Wall of China. If a man on the moon looked with naked eye down on this earth, the only man-made object he could detect would be that Wall."

We shifted our feet around in the sand, wondering why the chaplain had picked this particular time for this particular discourse. "Just look at it from here and let your imaginations come into play." We looked, but our imaginations remained dormant. We had been aware of the Wall's existence for a month or two, but still hadn't formed any definite conclusions. It was where it was, and we were where we were; and that seemed to be about the sum of it. "Now then," said the chaplain, "what would you say if you were offered the opportunity of going right up to it and getting a really good look at it? It's two thousand one hundred and fifty-six years old. It's the greatest man-made construction on the face of the earth. What would you say?" None of us said anything.

"I have planned such a trip," said the chaplain, "and I want some of you to come along with me. You can see from here how the Wall looks from *this* side. But what I intend to do is see how it looks from the *other* side. For the *other* side is the side you take to climb the mountain. And it's on the *other* side where the really magnificent view is available.

We'll go by train to Shanhaikwan and climb the mountain on the *other* side and get a really good look at the wonderful old thing. This is an opportunity you'll probably never have again in all your lives. Here are the details: We'll have to keep the first trip small, sort of feeling our way, as it were. Later on, after the problems have been worked out, I see no reason why an entire company shouldn't go. Now, those of you who want to make this first trip, just leave your names with your first sergeant. He and I will go over the list and see how many men we think we can manage on the first tryout. Your company commander is enthusiastic about the idea, and, naturally, so am I. Leave your names with your first sergeant, and I'll let the lucky ones know as soon as possible about the rest of the details."

When he came around the next day to pick up the names, he found that exactly five men had volunteered: Corporal Edward Brutschi, Private Digby Hand, Private Robert Counts, Private Calhoun Shaw, and myself, likewise a private. The chaplain was disappointed, but made an effort to hide his feelings. "Okay," he said. "Fine. Anything new around here always gets kicked in the teeth the first time you try it out. I wasn't ordering anybody; I was just asking. But this thing will catch on. I'm sure it will. You men are the pioneers, and I like the pioneering spirit. This shows you *want* to go. This shows you *want* to do something besides lie around on your bunks all the time. We will leave this camp Saturday morning at seven o'clock and entrain one hour later at Chingwangtao. I've arranged with your company commander for you to miss inspection and otherwise have the day off. I'll see you at seven Saturday morning, fellows, at the flagpole; and I promise you an interesting and instructive day."

Saturday morning at seven found us at the flagpole, freshly bathed and shaved, all dressed alike in laundered and pressed Hong Kong khaki shirts and slacks, black neckties tucked in at the second button, and neatly blocked campaign hats adorned with the blue infantry cord and the 15th Infantry's proud symbol—the dragon insigne bearing the regimental motto "Can Do."

We stood around in the sand, trying to keep the shine from leaving our shoes, and waiting for the chaplain. Instead of him, the Officer of the Day appeared. "The chaplain is ill," he said after he returned Corporal Brutschi's salute. "But he says he has complete faith in you, Brutschi, and he wants you to carry on without him. He says he's briefed you enough so you'll know what to do. Here's the money the chaplain had for your train fare."

"Yessir," said Brutschi, and the Officer of the Day left. And then Brutschi said to us, "I dunno whether we ought to go or not." Brutschi had been born in Poland; he spoke Middle Western English with a soft Polish accent. He also spoke Russian in addition to his native Polish, and he had picked up a working knowledge of Mandarin during his five years with the 15th.

"Course we'll go," said Digby Hand indignantly. "Lead off, Brutschi, 'fore somebody comes along and says not to. You got the chaplain's and the O.D.'s permission. What else you want?"

"Okay," said Brutschi. "I guess it's all right. Get in a column of twos. Let's go."

We left the camp and marched down the road that paralleled the beach. We could see a big green ocean liner tied up at the Kailan Mining Administration pier at Chingwangtao. We knew all about her. She was the *Empress of India*, out of Vancouver, making a stop on an Asiatic cruise. Most of the tourists aboard her had taken train to Peking to see the Temple of Heaven and the Forbidden City.

At Chingwangtao, we bought first-class passenger tickets on the Peking-Mukden Railway for the trip to Shanhaikwan. We pocketed them and strolled around, waiting for the train to pull in. An hour later, we discovered that the train would be five hours late. "Now then," said Brutschi, "we can either go back to the ticket seller's window and wreck the place, or we can climb on that coal train there that's ready to pull out and ride it to Shanhaikwan. The station agent says we can take it instead of waiting for the *wagon-lits*."

Little Shaw wanted to wreck the ticket seller's window and get his money back, but the rest of us decided that riding the coal train would be fun, and we overruled him. He had only been in China five months, and his opinions weren't to be bothered with.

We climbed up the rungs of an empty gondola spotted about three cars behind the locomotive, and jumped down inside. It was filthy with coal dust, and we were fearful that the dust would soil our uniforms. Brutschi hailed a near-by coolie and dickered with him to bring us some kaoliang mats such as were used to cover the cargo on flatcars. These mats, when the coolie delivered them, were nice and clean and about six feet by eight feet in size. We tied some of them to the inner sides of the gondola and spread others on the floor. We made ourselves a protected nook to ride in.

A vendor came along and sold us bottles of Japanese beer. We sipped the warm stuff and began to yell at the Chinese crew to start the coal train moving; we didn't want to be there all day. Chinese brakemen and switchmen in those days wore black gowns and straw hats shaped like inverted salad bowls. They blew loud whistles and waved flags, but nothing ever seemed to result from their activities. They yelled something back at us which Brutschi interpreted as meaning "Pretty soon train go when more people come." We didn't know what that meant, but in a few minutes a group of white civilians appeared along the track. There were three men and four women and three children. One of them—a woman—looked up at us in our coal car (we were lined up against a kaoliang mat, staring down at them) and she said in a perplexed voice, "Are you . . . are you . . . what are you?"

Private Digby Hand from Arkansas replied, "We're soldier boys, mam, from the U.S.A. Kin we help you any?"

She said, "Well, uh, I don't think so." And she and her companions drew off a little and conferred. "They're Canadians," said Counts. "Tourists off the *Empress of India.* They probably want to go to the Great Wall, too, only they don't know how to get there."

Then one of the men left the group and came to our car again and, shielding his eyes from the sun, looked up at us and said, "Are you men in charge of this train? Guards, or something of that nature?"

"No, sir," said Brutschi, who hadn't talked to a white civilian from North America for five years. "We're just passengers. We're going to Shanhaikwan to have a look at the Great Wall."

"Well, that's where we're bound, too," said the tourist. "We have our tickets. But isn't there supposed to be a passenger train, a *wagon-lits?* Surely not just a coal train."

"The *wagon-lits* has been delayed, sir," explained Brutschi. "It won't be along for four or five hours. That's why we got on this gondola. It'll leave in a few minutes. I guess you can ride with us, too. There's plenty of room."

"It seems so irregular," said the tourist. He went back into another conference with his companions.

Meanwhile, more black-gowned switchmen had appeared, and there was a great and concentrated blowing of whistles and waving of flags, and up ahead the locomotive began to hoot. It was obvious that something was going to happen at any minute.

The Canadians came to a vigorous decision. In a body, they marched to our coal car and, one after another, ascended the iron rungs. Some of the women were elderly and stout, but they were as spry at getting into the gondola as we young men had been. They took possession of our kaoliang-mat-lined nook and crowded us out of it. "How primitive," one of the women said. "But at least the railway was thoughtful enough to put these ridiculous mats in. I suppose we shall have to stand for the entire journey."

"Them's our mats," mumbled Brutschi, "but I guess you're welcome to 'em." And with that he retreated with the rest of us to the far end of the car and swore under his breath. We huddled in the middle, as much away from the grimy sides as we could get.

"What'll we do if we have to go to the bathroom?" whispered little Shaw anxiously. "You'll just have to hold it," said Brutschi. "Don't drink any more beer. Damn people. Why didn't they stay on their boat?"

Then the coal train's conductor came along the platform. He was dressed in a green uniform. He hoisted himself expertly into the car and began taking up and punching tickets as calmly as if we had been in the luxurious accommodations for which we had bought seats. The Canadians complained furiously to him, but, except for giving their tickets extra incisive punches, he paid no attention. When he had done with theirs and ours, he hopped from the car and trotted somewhere up ahead; and, in two minutes, without any further whistle-blowing or flag-waving, the coal train gave a savage lurch and we were on our way to Shanhaikwan.

It took us nearly an hour to make the twenty-five-mile trip. The Canadians either leaned comfortably against their mat-protected walls or crouched comfortably on their mat-protected floor. We men of Brutschi's command swayed and teetered in the middle of the gondola, half-clutching each other to keep from rubbing against the car's dirty sides. The scenery was undoubtedly magnificent—mountains and seascape and greenery—but we were too busy trying not to soil our uniforms to notice much of it. The Canadians chattered happily and became delighted with the novel ride, but little Shaw said, "I didn't wanta come on this damn coal train, Brutschi, but you went and made me." Corporal Brutschi said, "Oh, shut up." And Digby Hand said, "I'll let you buy me the first beer, kid, when we git to Shanhaikwan if you promise not to whine any more."

We disentrained in good order at Shanhaikwan's depot, having managed to keep our uniforms clean, but somehow in the process having missed noticing exactly how we got through the Great Wall. We waited for the Canadians to get off first, and hoped we would never see them again. "Now then," said Brutschi, "let's go to a bar or a restaurant or something and have a beer and lay out a campaign of action. The return train comes through at five this afternoon. It's only ten now, so we got practically all day."

He tilted back his Stetson campaign hat, put his hands on his hips, and looked around. "That there," he said, pointing to a wide street, "must be the road that goes up the mountain. Over there is shops and things, and, dammit, that looks like a hotel. We'll go there for our beer. Look at that damn Wall. It must be forty feet high."

"I don't think it's no wall at all," said Digby Hand. "I think it's part of the mountain, like something that growed out of it."

"Yeah, but it's got houses and things on it," said little Shaw. "I betcha if you had a truck and could get it on top you could drive the whole way on it."

"Those ain't houses," said Counts. "Those are crenellated parapets. The chaplain said so. I wrote it down."

"Ah, come on, Brutschi," said Hand. "Let's go git some beer. We got all day to look at the Wall."

The citizens of Shanhaikwan paid no more attention to us than if we had been a flock of chickens clucking and hopping along the streets. Shanhaikwan itself appeared to us as being an incredibly cluttered-up place, a sort of out-breaking and splattering around of the Great Wall itself, the debris and leftovers from it having been used in the construction of the city. Everything was gray: gray stone, gray brick, gray tile. The chaplain had told us that the Great Wall was the only reason for the city's existence. If the Wall hadn't started there, there would have been no city. Its name meant "Gate Between Mountain and Sea." The Wall, to quote the chaplain further, who I later discovered had quoted the Encyclopedia Britannica, "was the earliest architectural monument above the soil in China, and was one of the world's great constructions."

But, as Digby Hand had pointed out, we had all day to look at it, so Corporal Brutschi led us to what he had diagnosed as being a hotel, and we went in and found tables and sat down and ordered beer.

A white-gowned hotel boy served us, and then the proprietor came in. He was a Turk.

"Roff stoff," he said, "joost leetle beet roff stoff, end I call de shimboos. [Shimboos are Chinese police.] Last time vas sailors. Dey break my plates. Hot dam sumbishes. I hate. Solchers no better. Solchers vorse. Py Gott, joost leetle beet roff stoff end out you go on der ess. I varn you pastards. I varn you."

"How about some fried eggs?" asked Digby Hand. "I'm getting kinda hungry. How about cooking us up some eggs?"

"No, py Gott," said the Turk. "No eks I cook."

At this point, Corporal Brutschi began to talk to him in Russian, a tongue which the Turk understood better than he did English. Brutschi assured him we were well-behaved young men and wouldn't break his plates as the sailors had done, and that we had money and would pay for everything we ordered, but that we were hungry after our train ride and would like some fried eggs. The Turk was suspicious, but he finally gave the order to the boy; and after a while we were served with a huge platter of fried eggs, dozens of them. The Turk also let us have a big bowl of soda crackers to eat with them.

We were enjoying the eggs when the Canadians came in. They had been wandering around the city, had got lost, and had come to the hotel to get their bearings. The children they had with them saw us eating our eggs and began to pester the elders with cries of hunger. The Turk had thunder in his eyes as the Canadians sat down at the remaining tables and began to hector him about a menu.

"Eat up," said Brutschi. "Let's get out of here."

We returned to the streets of Shanhaikwan and walked about somewhat aimlessly. "This burg ain't a bit like Tientsin," said Digby Hand. "There ain't any beggars for one thing."

"Where are we at?" asked little Shaw.

"Kid, you're in China," said Counts. "Don't you remember?"

"I don't think I am," said Shaw. "I betcha I ain't. I betcha we're somewhere else. We come through the Wall, didn't we? Or around it or under it or something? Ain't the Wall the dividing line or something? I betcha we ain't in China no more."

"He's right," said Counts. "I had done forgot. We ain't in China no more. We're in Manchuria—a brand-new world. But it don't look any different."

A Manchurian in a blue gown approached us. "He's a pimp," said Counts. "I can tell 'em anywhere."

"American soldiers?" asked the Manchurian. "From the Chingwangtao camp? How nice. Some nice girls here in nice house. Russian. Clean. Very nice."

"No," said Brutschi. "Not today."

"Korean girls, too," said the Manchurian.

"Huh uh," said Brutschi.

"Japanese girls," said the Manchurian.

"Nope," said Brutschi.

"Aw, now wait, Brutschi!" protested little Shaw.

"No!" said Brutschi. "We come here to look at the Wall. And that's all. Now shut up."

The Manchurian said, "Proper way to see Wall is from top of mountain. You come this way, please. Donkeys available for ride up mountain. Come, I show you."

"Aw, heck, Brutschi!" cried little Shaw. "Cain't we just go *look* at them Japanese? Just *look*? That's all I mean, Brutschi."

"No," reiterated Brutschi. "We come to look at the Wall, and that's all. Now shut up." And he said to the Manchurian, "We don't need a guide."

"Very good," said the Manchurian. "This street goes to road up mountain. Donkeys available at stable. Welcome to Shanhaikwan."

"Okay," said Brutschi. "Come on, fellas." And he led off.

"Hell," said Shaw. "This ain't no fun at all. I druther be back in camp. You're worse'n a Sunday school teacher, Brutschi."

"Look, kid," said Digby Hand, "if you're just going to whine and beef all the time, what in the name of hell did you come along for, anyhow? Leave the rest of us enjoy ourselves, even if you cain't. Try being a good sport for onct, and not jest a damn spoiled brat."

"Well, it wouldn't hurt just to look at them Japanese," said Shaw. "Damned old Wall. Who cares about it?"

"Look, kid," said Brutschi, "when we get back to camp, the chaplain is going to ask us all kinds of questions about what we saw and so on, and so will the company commander. Well, suppose we say: Aw, we just seen some Japanese bims. Now wouldn't that look fine?"

"I don't care how it would look. That's what I *want* to do."

"Well, you cain't," said Counts. "So shut up about it."

The street we were on led to a sort of stable-like place, made as was everything in Shanhaikwan of gray stone, gray brick, and gray tile. And, as was everything else there, it was century upon century old—probably as old as the Wall itself. Indeed, it might once have sheltered the war horses of the mighty Emperor Ch'in Shih Huang Ti, who had given his name Ch'in to China, who had burned all the books and decreed that new ones be written, and who had ordered in 228 B.C. that the Great Wall be built and forever fix the boundaries of Cathay. Now, as we approached the stable, we saw it sheltered little Mongolian asses.

"Do them things carry you up that mountain?" asked Robert Counts. For he was from Missouri where the mules grew big and strong, and these onagers came only up to his waist, and their legs were thinner than his wrists; and the mountain reared so steeply that you had to tilt your head back to look at it properly.

"I'd jest as soon walk," said Digby Hand. "I ain't clum a mountain in many a day now, and I'm raring to give my shanks a workout. You guys saddle up on them there thoroughbreds if you want to. I'll race you for the beer."

Corporal Brutschi dickered with the donkey boys at the stable. "It's a dollar Mex for the trip up and back. Sounds kind of steep to me. You guys want to ride or walk?"

"I'm walking, like I done said," said Hand. "I figure walking's better than dragging my feet from one of those critters."

"Well, I ain't," said Shaw. "I'm riding. I want that gray one, Brutschi."

Counts and I decided to ride, too. Brutschi said he would walk with Digby Hand.

The Great Wall went straight up the side of the mountain with a shocking starkness of line, but its accompanying road shooflied back and forth so as not to exhaust the man or beast which might be traveling it. Even so, it was still bitterly steep. The ruts in it were more than two thousand years old. What hell the wall builders had encountered in piling their stones up the side of that mountain in the first place could only be imagined, but it must have served to toughen them for the fifteen hundred miles which lay ahead.

The Mongolian asses were equipped with wooden saddle boards covered with cotton. These saddle boards, being perfectly flat on top, conformed not at all to the configuration of a man. It hurt just to sit on them without moving; when the donkeys began their ascent of the rutted, iron-hard road, it became torture. There were no stirrups to put one's feet in; there were no reins to hold. One sat upon the board and clutched the edges of it, and leaned far forward so as not to slip off and roll back down the mountain. Each little beast was led by a donkey boy; and each step they took seemed beast's and boy's last. Up ahead at the third shoofly was a dainty little stone teahouse that looked like a pagoda. "They got beer there," said Brutschi. "Last man to reach it has got to pay for all."

This was the first of the races we staged up that awful road. Digby Hand won it, and all the others, easily. He was six-feet-two and as thin as a mop handle, and looked not at all like a mountain climber. But he stretched himself forward until the tip of his snipelike nose almost touched the steep road surface ahead of him, and he pumped his long, skinny legs up and down like pistons. Against him, the Mongolian asses had not a chance. The race up to that first teahouse took its toll. My beast was not worn out, but I was. When we reached the pagoda, I paid off my donkey boy and told him to take himself and his animal back to the stables. Counts made a similar decision, and thereafter little Shaw was the only mounted man on the expedition.

At that first teahouse, a very old and very amiable Man-churian sold us Dairen beer. It was nicely chilled. And there, sitting on the stone steps, we began to look around. There was much to see: Wall, mountain, city, gulf, immensity.

"I don't want this here beer," said little Shaw. "Whudja order it for? I want some soda pop."

Brutschi, loser of the race to the teahouse, got him some pop from the Manchurian, and the rest of us finished Shaw's opened bottle between us. Counts, who had been staring down the road, said, "Well, here come our friends." And we looked where he pointed, and there were the Canadians, riding up from the stables. "Drink up," said Brutschi. "Let's get going."

So we tackled the road again, and it was steeper than ever, and the crest of the mountain seemed as far up and away as it ever had been; and finally Counts said, "What in hell *are* we doing this for? We don't *hafta* climb this mountain. I'm getting like Shaw: I don't care nothing about the damn Wall. I druther be back down in Shanhaikwan with them Japanese girls than climbing this damn crazy steep thing."

Said Corporal Brutschi patiently, "The chaplain told us to come and see what the Wall was like. If he hadn't of got sick and could of come along with us, he would be here now and we would be climbing this mountain just like we are now. And if the chaplain was here, there wouldn't be no talk about Japanese girls. And you know it, Counts."

"Yes, but he *ain't* here, Brutschi. That's the difference."

"There ain't any difference, Counts. I got my orders to carry out just as if he *was* here."

"I don't get it," said Counts.

Little Shaw twisted around on his saddle board and said, "Well, I get it. Brutschi's just an old Sunday school teacher, like I said down in Shanhaikwan, but nobody wouldn't listen to me. The chaplain said we was to come so's to look at the Wall from the other side and see what it was like. Well, we're on the other side, but it ain't no different from the front side 'cept it seems like there's more of it. What we gonna do when we get to the top of the mountain, Brutschi? That's what I wanta know."

Brutschi did not seem too sure himself. "Well, we can look around. Temples, and things like that."

"Temples!" said Shaw.

"Quit whining and keep going," said Digby Hand. "The Canadians is ketching up on us. Don't let it never be said thet a bunch of old women and men and kids kin beat the Can Do outfit up the side of a mountain. Come on, boy; lay the switch to thet there race hoss of yours."

We passed the next teahouse without stopping, for it really looked as if the Canadians were catching up. All of them were mounted, and they rode in a determined group; and they were only two shooflies below us. Sound travels upward: We could hear their querulous, complaining voices, but could not make out the words.

Even little Shaw sensed that some vague issue of honor was at stake. We quickened our pace as much as we could, and somehow managed to widen the distance between our party and the Canadians. But it took a lot of effort. "I don't see how them old bags do it," said Counts. "But I guess they come from the hills or something and are used to it. Look at that one in the lead. You can't even see her donkey on account of her skirts and things. She looks like she was coming up the mountain on some kind of chair."

We reached the top. We were short of wind and aching of limb, and our Hong Kong khaki shirts were sweaty, but we had made it and we had beaten the Canadians by a good fifteen minutes. The road ended at an aerie of stone and tile, a temple-like random place of stone stairs, stone bannisters, tile roofs, stone floors on different levels, and stone demons, lions, and dogs. On those stone porches, you could stand and look and see the Great Wall flow up and down and on into the Jehol Mountains, always selecting the highest peak over which to pour.

On one of the more secluded porches, we found some tables and chairs and concluded it was another teahouse. An attendant appeared; we ordered beer. Again it was Dairen beer, nicely chilled. And Digby Hand said, "I'm kinda hungry. Ask the guy, Brutschi, if he kin cook us up some eggs."

"Aw, no," said little Shaw. "I ain't gonna eat no more damn eggs. Why, we ain't et nothing else all day. We had 'em for breakfast, and then we went and had 'em again at that hotel. I ain't eating no more eggs, Brutschi. I just ain't."

"I like eggs," said Hand. "I kin eat 'em any old time."

Brutschi said to Shaw, "I'll getcha something else, kid." And he spoke to the attendant, and the attendant nodded and went off. "Whudja order?" asked Shaw suspiciously.

"Can of sardines," said Brutschi.

As we were drinking our beer and eating our eggs and Shaw was eating his sardines, the Canadians came upon us again.

One of the women said, "Every time we see these soldiers they are drinking beer and eating eggs. Don't they ever do anything else in the American Army?"

The Canadian small fry came up to our table and looked hungrily at our fare. "C'mon," muttered Brutschi to us. "Eat up. Let's go."

We took a path that led away from the aerie and curved around under the cedars and finally ended abruptly at the Wall itself. We sat down on a stone bench; the Wall cast its shadow upon us.

"Well," said Counts, "is this it? Is this all we do?"

"I reckon," said Brutschi. "Unless you want to walk around some more and do some more looking."

"Well, I don't," said Shaw. "I've seen every damn thing I wanta see 'cept them Japanese girls." He picked up a stone fragment and began to chip at the Wall. "Cut it out," said Brutschi crossly.

"Aw, I ain't hurting it none," said Shaw. "I'm just putting my name on it. Lookee: SHAW 1928. Now, if somebody comes along ten jillion years from now, they'll know that I've been here and when it was. This wall ain't so tough. I betcha I can dig a big hunk out of it." And he chipped away with his shard and managed to dislodge a flake of mortar.

His undertaking was catching. We all—even Corporal Brutschi—picked up stone fragments and began to attack the Wall. It was fun.

When we had finished, we had made quite a scratch on its surface.

Then Digby Hand said: "Look, Brutschi, this jest ain't getting anywhere. We have clum the mountain, and we have seen the Wall, everything like the chaplain said. But ain't it time we had a little fun on our hook? Whatya say, Brutschi? Let's git offen this mountain and take a look at them Japanese girls. We ain't got too much time left."

"That's what I been saying all along," said little Shaw.

"Me, too, kind of," said Counts.

"Well, I dunno," said Brutschi. "But I guess so. I guess we've seen as much as we should of up here."

Invigorated, we sprang up from the stone bench. "Lead the way, Corporal Brutschi," said Digby Hand from Arkansas. "Jest lead the way."

Brutschi led, and we ran straight into one of the Canadians, one of the men Canadians. He wore plus fours and had a camera slung around his neck.

"You're just the men I'm looking for," he said. "You fellows move around so fast there's no keeping up with you. I have a very grave favor to ask of you. You, Corporal, are the leader, aren't you?"

"Yes, sir," said Brutschi doubtfully.

"Well, now," said the the Canadian, "then I suppose that the Chinese policeman in the teahouse alerted you, didn't he?"

"Policeman?" said Brutschi. "We never saw no policeman."

"Oh, he probably came up the mountain after you left the teahouse. You fellows are harder to keep up with than a herd of mountain goats. Anyhow, he said there was a bandit report out, and it would be best for us to get back down to Shanhaikwan as soon as possible. Nothing serious, you know. Just a vague report. But, uh, well, the ladies in my party would feel more secure if you chaps would accompany us on the way down. You know how women are; these bandit reports spook 'em. That's the favor I want to ask of you. You are about to leave, aren't you? Well, be good chaps and come along with us. Nothing formal about it, you know. But the ladies would feel so much safer. Of course, I discount this bandit talk. I fought at Vimy Ridge, you know. But you know how ladies are."

"Yeah, but we ain't got any guns or anything," said Brutschi.

"Oh, but we know that, Corporal! We realize the . . . uh . . . limitations. But just to have American soldiers along; you know that would give the ladies such a boost."

"Well, I guess so," said Brutschi. "The chaplain never said nothing about bandits, but I guess it's okay."

"Good!" said the Canadian. "I don't know how to thank you. Perhaps with a beer in Shanhaikwan, eh?"

"Aw, you won't be owing us nothing," said Brutschi.

So, casting our eyes nervously about for bandits, we convoyed the Canadians down the mountain, a trip which, if anything, was more taxing than the ascent. Little Shaw rode among the tourists on his sure-footed Mongolian ass. Brutschi, Hand, Counts, and I labored on foot down those interminable stone shooflies. A new set of muscles had to be brought into play. A new set of aches developed. Shaw became quite friendly with the Canadians, particularly with the women. "Nice, animated little chap, isn't he?" said the plus-four man to me as I slid down the road beside his donkey. "Yes, he is," I said. "He's been the life of our party all day."

"What I admire about you chaps," said the Canadian, "is your youth. Take the Wall, for instance. It's old and all that, but I say damn the Wall. Give me youth any time."

"Yessir," I said.

No bandits appeared then or at any other time, although it is true there were many bandits operating in Manchuria in those days. The Canadians insisted on buying us some beer in the Turk's hotel while we waited for the train to take us back to Chingwangtao. We said we really didn't want any. And that was the truth, for what we really wanted was to go and look at the Japanese girls. But the Canadians had us surrounded and were adamant about buying us beer. We couldn't get away.

One of the women took the Turk innkeeper aside and whispered to him. When the train pulled in, she said, "I've got a surprise for you boys. To eat on the way back." She handed Brutschi a paper bag.

He opened it after we took our seats in the *wagon-lits.* It contained a dozen hard-boiled eggs.

THE RATEL HUNT

4

Another summer, the squad I was in had won, by its proficiency, the right to represent E Company in the annual competition for the Chief of Infantry's Cup. We were known officially as E Company's Chief of Infantry Combat Squad. Our battalion, the Second, had finished its summer stay at Chingwangtao and was back in Tientsin. The Third Battalion occupied the camp, and when each company there had selected its Combat Squad, the Combat Squads of the Second Battalion were sent down to compete with them for the Cup. There were no trains running then on the Peking-Mukden line, some warlording affair having interfered, and we went down on a little coastal steamer named the *Gerthe*. Something was wrong with the *Gerthe*'s rudder and, instead of going in a straight line, we went wiggle-waggle all the way through the Gulf of Pei Chih-li. It was around the first of August when we arrived at camp, and it was not until six weeks later that we returned to Tientsin, for it was only then that another boat became available to bring us back.

The first week was spent by our squad and the others in practice for Cup competition. The practice runs and the grand event itself took place on the rifle range. The runs, when done by well-trained men, were beautiful things to watch. After we had taken our turn at one, we would sit off on a sand dune to the side of the range and watch the other squads work out. Very few civilians have ever seen Combat Cup squads in action. I do not even know that the exercise is being done any more by the infantry, the weapons having changed so much since the old China days.

After the Cup competition was over, our squad having come out second, we had nearly five weeks of absolutely nothing to do. The Third Battalion was waiting for a boat to take it back to Tientsin, and we, perforce, waited with it. We were quartered with I Company and had our own squad tent. We ate in I Company's mess and were shaved by I Company's barbers, and our beds were made and our shoes shined by I Company's coolies; but there the relationship ended. There was just no place to fit us in. We had already completed our own summer training. All that I Company was doing was killing time on maneuvers until the boat should arrive. The I Company commander saw no point in marching us out with his own men. So we had more than a month of nothing to do except eat and sleep. Being soldiers, we loved it. Five members of the squad, including the corporal, made the most of it. They said they were catching up on the energy they had expended in the Combat Cup runs. They got up in the morning, ate breakfast, then hit their bunks again, snitching magazines to read from vacant I Company tents while the occupants were away on some aimless hike or even more aimless field problem.

Martin Lord, Digby Hand, and I were of a more restless

nature. We explored. We walked down the beach to Pei-
taho, the summer resort fifteen miles away, stared at the
white missionary families there in their cottages, and came
back to camp on a freight train. We made forays to the
edge of forbidden Chingwangtao, and were ordered away
from its gates by the MPs stationed there. We settled with
drinking beer at Hop Kee's, a ship chandler outside of Chingwangtao proper. When the Third Battalion went one way,
we went another. We visited little inland Chinese villages,
each one snug behind its pretty stone wall. Martin Lord by
then could speak Mandarin so proficiently that he wore the
honored *chung*, on his sleeve, the regimental emblem of
mastery in the Chinese language.

It was Digby Hand who proposed that we should go on
a hunting expedition. "Where's them places," he asked,
"where Zorgaleski took General Castner that time, and
they pot-shotted all the woodcocks and Zorgy got made
high private?"

"Oh, it's that strip of trees the KMA planted for erosion
control," said Martin Lord. "Where Chang Doe and his
father live. We've been through there half a dozen times
and not seen anything. The general must have cleaned out
all the wild game."

"Well, I crave to hunt something," said Digby. "Not jest
birds, neither. Animals, big-game animals; that's what I
crave."

"There aren't any big-game animals around here," said
Martin Lord. "Kublai Khan killed the last tiger on New
Year's Eve of 1270. Besides, what are you going to use for
gun?"

"Maybe the supply sergeant would loan us a Springfield."

We really sneered at that. The supply sergeant of I Company wouldn't lend a broken crutch to his crippled grand-
mother.

We were about six miles inland from camp, lolling on

a knoll in a countryside that looked like a well-kept park, when this significant conversation took place. A streamlet purled around the foot of the knoll. Some cattle grazed under scattered trees. We had brought along some beer and sardines from Jawbone Charlie's *peng*. "Let's tear into the picnic lunch," said Martin Lord, and he opened a bottle of beer.

It was then that we saw the Chinese hunter. He was a very young hunter, about fifteen or sixteen, and he carried an extraordinarily long shooting iron. He didn't see us. He coursed about somewhat like a hound, stopping often to peer. A rabbit jumped out of a clump of grass, hopped for about fifty feet, then stopped and looked back at the hunter. The lad brought his fantastic weapon up to his shoulder, aimed, fired, fell back a foot or two from the recoil, then stared through the blanket of smoke to see what he had achieved. The rabbit, a very small one, lay dead upon the greensward. Digby Hand, Martin Lord, and I cheered.

We went down the knoll to congratulate the nimrod, and were met with a big grin of triumph and a little dance of glee. With him we examined, and exulted over, the rabbit. Martin Lord found that he and the lad could understand patches of what the other was saying in Mandarin. I was interested in the rabbit because I had never seen a Chinese hare before. But Digby Hand was enthralled by the hunter's weapon. "Ask him to lemme look at it, Martin," he kept saying. The youth, when he understood what was wanted, happily did so, and Digby let out a howl of incredulity. "It's the same damn gun my grandpap toted in the Civil War," he almost shouted. "I mean it's the same model."

Martin and I scoffed.

"Looka here," said Digby. "Looka here, if you don't believe me." And he pointed to the lock plate. There, as plain as day, was the inscription: "Cook & Brother, Athens, Ga.," the date 1862, and a serial number. And behind the hammer on the lock plate was an engraving of the Confederate flag.

"Don't tell me I don't know this here gun when I see it," said Digby. "It's the same shooting iron Grandpap toted in the Civil War, and he brought his'n home with him when the war was over. He was in the cavalry, but when they run out of hosses they made him an infantryman and gave him a Cook's musket to pack. I shot his'n many a time when I was a kid. He still claims it's the best firearm ever made." And Digby began to do the Confederate rifle drill with the antique piece, and the young Chinese hunter laughed and clapped his hands.

"Come on, Digby, let us have a look at it, too," said Martin Lord.

Digby handed it over reluctantly; we hefted it and aimed it and tried out its trigger pull, and ended up by admiring it and coveting it. It was the Class I infantry rifle of the Confederate armies, .58 caliber, with a 33-inch barrel. Three

bands of brass secured the barrel to the full-length stock. It
was built on the Enfield model, and had a ramrod inserted
in the stock just under the barrel. Both sights were fixed,
the front sight doing double duty as a bayonet lug. It was
a single-shot muzzle-loader, of course, and its hammer was
big enough to drive nails with. The amazing thing about it
was that it was still in perfect shape. The stock was
scratched, the metal parts worn in places, but there it was
—as efficient as the day it had left Cook and Brother's
arsenal.

It was undeniably clumsy as compared with our 1903
bolt-action Springfields, but, undeniably, too, it had a rugged grace about it and a businesslike, no-fooling appearance
that was singularly impressive. I looked at the little rabbit it
had just killed. Cook and Brother were long dead. The war
the rifle had fought in was long over. The soldiers the gun
had killed were long gone. But here was the rifle, as alive as
it ever had been, as eager as it ever was to kill some more.

"They're indestructible damn things, I'm telling you,"
said Digby.

Martin Lord questioned the young Chinese about it.
Where had he gotten it? "In family long time," said the
boy, proud that he possessed something which interested the
American soldiers. "Ancestor get from man on ship. Ship
with sails. Only oldest son allowed to hunt with honored
gun. I now oldest son."

Digby Hand looked at the dead rabbit critically. "Thet
there bunny wasn't killed with no Minié ball, Martin," he
said. "Ask the kid what kind of loads he's using and whur
he gits 'em."

Martin questioned the youth. "It's sort of mixed up," he
said finally. "Something about a firecracker man. But apparently this firecracker man sells powder and percussion
caps in Chingwangtao." The hunter listened intently and
wagged his head in agreement, although obviously he didn't

understand English. But such is the sympathy between people interested in the same thing that he caught the drift well
enough. He carried at his waist a brass powder flask and a
pouch. He opened the pouch and showed the contents to
Digby. It was bird shot, about BB size. "Good God!" said
Hand. "He's using the thing fer a shotgun. He's ruining
the bore." And he snatched the rifle from the boy and looked
into the muzzle. "Maybe he ain't," he conceded. "I kin still
see the lands and grooves. But this does it, Martin. I aim to
fire this here piece at live game. I usta kill muskrats with
Grandpap's—damn near blow 'em apart—and my hunting
instinct is raring to go again. Ask the kid if he's got any
big bullets—you know, the regular .58 caliber slugs."

Martin asked. The boy knew what he meant, but shook
his head. "All gone. Years gone."

"Well, then, has he got a bullet mold?"

Martin took that up with the youth, and again the
youth understood. From his pouch, he took out a small
hand mold.

"Ask him if we kin borry it long enough to make some
bullets."

The youth seemed to anticipate this. "He says yes," said
Martin, "if you will teach him the dance with the rifle. He
means, of course, the Confederate manual of arms."

"Teach him!" said Digby. "I'll make him the best one-
man drill team since the days of the Louisiana Tigers."

And Martin Lord and I lay back in the grass and finished
the beer and watched while Digby Hand taught the young
Chinese hunter how to handle the musket as it was handled
in the days of Beauregard, Jackson, and Lee.

We made an agreement with the youth, and sealed it by
giving him two packs of cigarettes, to meet him there in the
same spot the next day, he to bring along his rifle and
powder flask and percussion caps, and we to bring some
proper .58 caliber bullets.

We went back to camp, Digby bearing the precious bullet mold. All we had to do was find some lead somewhere, melt it, pour it into the mold, and presto! Minié balls.

The catch was in finding lead. I Company's supply sergeant, when we diffidently approached him, told us to go dig for it if we wanted it so badly; he certainly didn't have any. Then Digby Hand remembered something, and he dug into his barracks bag and came up with a little statue of a Chinese god, assisted by a bull, performing a fertility rite with a surprisingly complacent Chinese maiden. "Bought it in the Jap Concession," he explained. "But I'd be kinda scared to take it home with me. We'll melt her down. If it ain't lead, it's mighty close to being lead. Feel how heavy it is." And he tossed it to Martin Lord. "Up in Peking," said Lord, examining it, "there's a life-size statue of the same thing in one of the temples. I saw some women tourists looking at it. They were quite interested. Said it represented some sort of sacrifice."

"Well, we'll sacrifice it fer bullets," said Digby. "Come on, let's git us a skillet."

We went into I Company's kitchen and browbeat the lone mess coolie there into letting us take a small frying pan. Then we stopped at Jawbone Charlie's *peng* and picked up some beer and went on to the KMA railway tracks. We gathered up tiny pieces of coal along the tracks and went under the concrete culvert where Chang Doe had set up shop with our stolen shoes. There we made a fireplace of rocks and made a fire in it. Digby put the frying pan on the fire, cut up the statue with Martin's Boy Scout knife, and dropped the pieces into the pan. By bending down and blowing into the coals, we achieved a forced draft effect. When the bottom of the frying pan became red-hot, the pieces of the statue began to melt and run together. Using all our handkerchiefs to protect his fingers, Digby took up the pan and attempted to pour the molten god into the mold. He was so nervous that he botched the first try and the second, but at length he came up with a perfect bullet. We crowed with delight and had a bottle of beer apiece in celebration. Then we went back to camp, returned the frying pan, and waited for supper. We had walked about twenty miles that day and were hungry, having had nothing to eat since breakfast except some sardines.

The question we debated that night as we lay on our cots in our squad tent was where to hunt, and what. Digby insisted that we seek out something larger and more ferocious than rabbits. At this point, I thought of something. There was a place I had heard about, and it had an animal in it which I wanted to see. The place was a graveyard; the animal was something which lived among the tombs.

Our company barber had told me about it when E Company proper had been in camp at the beginning of summer. I had been sitting in the barber chair, getting a haircut and thumbing through a copy of *Field and Stream.* In it was an illustrated article on hunting in India, and one of the illustrations was of a ratel, a badger-like animal which lives in India and Africa. The barber, who made a practice of looking over one's shoulder when one was looking at a magazine, saw the picture of the ratel and sniffed. "Hah! Little one. Chinese more bigger."

"You mean there's ratels in China?" I asked.

"Sure in China. But big, big. No little like this one. Big. Bad, too. Very bad."

"What's so bad about them?"

"Eat dead people. Live all time in graveyards. Bad. We call grave robber."

"Oh, you mean those dogs that hang around the fishing village."

"No! Dogs we call *gravediggers.* This we call *grave robber.* Different, see?" And he said the words slowly in Chinese, but I couldn't tell any difference.

"Are there any around here?" I asked.

"In camp? Hah, hah! No find in camp. Only in graveyard. All time live in graveyard. Eat dead people. Very bad."

"Well, are there any graveyards around here?"

"Sure. Is big one Chingwangtao people use. Many years old. Over there." And he pointed vaguely with his scissors.

So, lying on my bunk that night, I remembered this, and I said to Digby Hand and Martin Lord, "Let's go to the Chingwangtao graveyard and Digby can shoot a grave robber." And I explained to them what a grave robber was. They were all for it.

"But where at is the graveyard?" asked Digby, tossing his bullet back and forth in his hands.

"The kid with the gun will know," I said.

"I'll act as a beater," said Martin, "and drive all the ratels in the cemetery toward you, Digby, and you can shoot the one with the biggest horns."

Next morning, we rendezvoused with the young hunter on the knoll where he had shot the hare. He was as happy as a monkey and insisted on doing the Confederate manual of arms for us for about ten minutes. "You're getting good at it, kid," said Digby, "but don't wear yourself out. Ask him where the graveyard is at, Martin."

Martin asked, and briefly sketched in our project. The young hunter's face took on a strange look. He didn't shake his head, but he said something which sounded like a warning.

"He says evil spirits live among the dead," said Martin.

We had brought along a barracks bag with us, and had stopped at Jawbone Charlie's *peng* and put in it bottles of beer and cans of sardines and a box of crackers. Digby took out a bottle of beer and opened it. "Tell him," he said, "the spirits in this here bottle is more pahrful than the spirits in the graveyard. Tell him to lead the way, Martin, and not to fear nothing. Wait a minute! Tell him to gimme thet gun.

I want her loaded and locked before I tackle grave robbers."

The youth handed over the old musket and stood by to appraise Digby's technique. Digby had learned the musket-loading art from a man whose life had once depended on how well the job was done, and he gave us a demonstration of efficiency.

The powder flask had a measuring device in its nozzle to insure the right amount of powder being used. Digby squinted at the calibration and set it at four drams. "Jest like you was loading a twelve-gauge shotgun," he explained. He poured the powder down the barrel. He took his bullet and seated it in the rifle's muzzle on a small patch of oily cloth. Then he took the ramrod, set the cupped end of it over the nose of the bullet, and, with a clean thrust, drove the bullet backward down the bore of the rifle and seated it firmly on top of the powder in the breach. He took a percussion cap from the little metal box the boy carried and fixed the cap on the nipple of the musket. He set the big hammer at half-cock. "Now," he said, "she's loaded fer bear. Lead on, young sprout, and keep yer eyes peeled fer signs of game."

The graveyard lay beyond the sand dunes and beyond some old entrenchments where warlords once had fought. It was away from the farming and grazing land proper and was situated on a stretch of flaky soil which I think now was loess, or something very like loess. It had a mud wall around it, a wall, which when we saw it was about two feet high, but which certainly had once been much higher and now was weathered away. The Chinese in that part of their country buried their dead in wooden coffins. They placed the coffins on top of the ground and piled dirt over them, each tomb becoming an elongated mound about waist-high. For some reason, in the area where the graveyard was, very little rain fell, the clouds following the mountains to the south and the coastline to the east. Probably that was why the site had been chosen for a burial ground in the first place.

It was old, incredibly old. The original Chingwangtao had been town-sited about 200 or 300 B.C., and a graveyard had been as much of a necessity then as in the following centuries. This one covered perhaps twenty acres; vestiges of a vastly earlier mud wall could be seen. Flattened-out mounds indicated very ancient tombs. Not quite so flattened-out heaps with shreds of wood still visible indicated the ones less ancient. Over the centuries in that rainless waste, new coffins had been placed on the mounds where old coffins had fallen away, and new dirt mounds had been erected on fallen-away mounds, the whole building up, century by century, into a kind of low hill. The place had a smell of its own. "Bad spirits here," said the young hunter.

"It's a good place fer 'em," said Digby Hand.

We could perceive no vegetable or animal life at all. There was only the eroded mud wall, the vestige of the former wall, and the forest of earthen tombs, each containing in its center —like a dead cocoon—its own dead. "Gives yuh the creeps," said Digby.

We were the only persons there, there being no funeral in progress that day. The newer mounds were located around the far borders of the wall, and there were signs that an extension of the wall was being planned—to make room, probably, for another century or two of dead. In the graveyard's center, the hill effect was particularly noticeable, the clustered, flattened, individual mounds rising almost to a peak of their own. It looked as if no one had been entombed in the center of the graveyard for hundreds of years. We saw a fresh new grave just outside the wall, the earth which covered the coffin being of the color of still freshly dug dirt. All around, little wheel-shaped pieces of paper lay scattered, each piece having a hole in its center. The idea was that if an evil spirit wanted to bedevil the cadaver, it would first have to make its way through all the individual holes in all those little wheels of paper, a task, the mourners hoped, beyond even the most diligent of imps.

I had no yearning to penetrate to the middle of the grave-yard where the hill effect was most prominent, but I pointed out to Digby and Martin Lord that if, indeed, ratels inhabited the place, they would probably have their burrows in the center, away from the traffic, as it were, on the weird hill where no one seemed to venture any more. If there was such a colony of animals, and if they did sustain themselves on the flesh of dead Chinese, and if they did live in burrows, the only place they could burrow was under the mounds. So, I said, as cheerfully as I could manage, let's go to the middle and have a good old look-see.

The young Chinese hunter was distressed and sought to dissuade us. "Bad place, bad place," he said to Martin Lord. "We know it," said Martin. "Tell you what: You find us a grave robber out here around the edges, and we won't go to the middle. Look around for grave-robber signs, why don't you?"

The young hunter almost neighed in scorn at our blindness. "Spoor everywhere." And he pointed to a grave mound that might have been a year old, or ten—there was no way of telling. At any rate, the dirt covering one end of the wooden coffin had been clawed away, and a hole had been gnawed in the coffin itself, as if by a giant rodent.

"He's right about the signs," said Digby. "Ain't thet a trail wandering off there—leading toward the center?"

It was hard to tell whether it was a trail or just some queer little channel the loess particles had made of themselves, perhaps at the urging of a wind gust. Loess, on the surface, is as unstable as the sea.

"Follow it," said Martin Lord. "Let's find out, and then let's *get out*. I'm sick of this damned place."

So Martin and Digby and I followed the little trail, but the young Chinese hunter held back. The trail led up the gentle, lumpy rise of the hill itself.

We never reached the top of the hill. We found the ghoul when we were only about halfway. It sat at the mouth of its burrow among grave mounds so old that they had almost flattened off to the level of the ground itself. It was cleaning itself, as does a dog, trying, while we watched it, to clear some matted stuff from its foreclaws.

Martin Lord had spotted it first. "There!" he whispered to Digby. "There!" And he pointed. The creature kept on trying to cleanse itself. Digby cocked and raised the Civil War musket to his shoulder and took aim. He held his aim for a long while. Then, abruptly, he lowered the weapon. "I cain't add no more dead to this place," he said. And he did something I had never seen him do before; he made the Sign of the Cross.

Our spirits had risen again when we reached the parklike place where we had first encountered the young hunter. We sat on the knoll and shared with him our beer, our crackers, and our sardines.

Digby said, "I still aim to fire this here thing. Pace off fifty yards, Martin, and set up a beer bottle. I'll see if my shooting eye is still prime."

Martin stood up the bottle as Digby directed. Digby took the same shooting position he would have had he been using his regular .30-06 Springfield. There was a roar and a cloud of black smoke. The bottle lay in smithereens.

I have never been able absolutely to identify the grave robber. In size it was somewhere between a badger and a wolverine, and was colored a peculiar gray on top and black underneath. Of course, its fur was very, very matted, but I do not think that was its natural state. It had not, in its appearance, seemed a very vicious animal. But where it lived its isolated life there was nothing to be very vicious about.

Taps

3 ✳

PRIVATE PRINCE

1

At eight on that April morning we formed a big horse-shoe inside our Compound and said good-by to our departing comrades as they circled self-consciously before us on their last parade. They circled twice, then swung out the Compound gate, with shoulders squared, and marched the miles to Tientsin East. There they boarded a train for Ching-wangtao, where the American Army transport *U. S. Grant* waited to take them back to the States. Their term of enlistment was almost up. They would be discharged from the army on their arrival at the presidio in San Francisco. As they left the Compound, which had been their home for almost three years, the Chinese clustered at the gate set off firecrackers—a parting salute. The marching men cheered.

At five o'clock that afternoon, we again formed a horse-shoe in the Compound, this time to welcome the newcomers replacing the old-timers who had left that morning. Their trains had passed each other on the Peking-Mukden Railway halfway between Tientsin and Chingwangtao. Our old squadmates would occupy the bunks that the newcomers had abandoned on the *U. S. Grant*. The newcomers would occupy the bunks that the old-timers had abandoned in our barracks. The Chinese, again clustered at the Compound gate, set off firecrackers to greet the new arrivals. The new arrivals shied like a herd of frightened animals.

When the old-timers had left that morning, they had been as polished and pressed and button-gleaming as any troops ever on formal parade. The new men who marched in were as rumpled and soiled as a gang of hobos. A hundred and twenty old-timers had marched out. A hundred and thirty new men marched in to take their places. We old China hands looked at the recruits critically and wondered which ones we would draw for our squadmates.

They straggled into our Compound, admonished by a detail of our non-commissioned officers, which had met them at Tientsin East and had chivied them through the streets of the city's foreign Concessions. Twice they were marched around inside our welcoming horseshoe; then they were halted and sorted out, some for this company, some for that. It was obvious that the awful, pervading smell of Tientsin distressed their nostrils. The wind-borne dust from the far-off Gobi Desert distressed their eyes. We called out to them and guyed them and jeered at them. All of them were young and all appeared most dispirited. A few of them snarled back.

Eleven of them were assigned to my company, and one of them, Private Prince, to the squad I was in. He was a heavyset, bushy-haired youth, thick of arm and leg and trunk—almost treelike in appearance. His face bore an expression such as might be detected in the bark of an elm. Martin Lord, senior first-class private and acting corporal in place of Brutschi who had gone home on the *U. S. Grant*, helped him get settled. Lord showed him his bunk and his foot locker and wall locker, told him where the showers were and where the mess hall was.

"Put away your stuff and go get washed," Lord told him. "Shave. Comb your hair. Put on a necktie. They're going to feed you new guys in a few minutes now. Hot pork sandwiches and lots of gravy and rice. You'll like it after that chow they fed you on the transport."

"I ain't hungry," Prince said.

"Ah, you've got to be hungry," Lord protested. "You haven't had anything to eat since you left the *Grant* this morning."

"I ain't hungry," he repeated.

Lord shrugged. "Nobody's forcing you to eat," he said.

To make conversation, I asked the newcomer, "How was the trip over? Did you get very seasick?"

"What do you mean?"

"Oh, throwing up and all—you know."

He thought awhile. "I never did nothing like that," he finally said.

The new men, although assigned to individual squads, were given recruit drill in a separate body—the "bolo brigade," we called it. Some of the men either had had previous training or were so quick to learn that they were taken out of the bolo brigade in a week or less and assigned to regular duty. But Private Prince boloed for a solid month, and even at the end of that time the non-coms who had been screaming at him daily had profound misgivings about his fitness for the simple tasks of soldiering.

"He still can't tell his left hand from his right," complained Acting Corporal Lord, who had been drilling the recruits and bucking for his corporal's stripes at the same time. "I've seen a lot of dumb oxes, but that animal's got them all beat. You can cuss at him, you can yell at him, you can get down on your knees and beg at him, but it still doesn't do any good."

The month's time allotted to training the bolos was up, however, and, competent or no, Private Prince became one of us in our garrison routine. He brought our squad's efficiency down to the lowest level it had ever suffered, and Martin Lord's achievement of corporal's stripes was thereby delayed, for Captain Hauser, the company commander, decided that, since the squad made such a poor showing, Lord obviously lacked the fiber required in a non-commissioned officer. Prince was incredibly awkward at drill, and he couldn't look neat even after he received his tailored uniform. His hair had grown so long during the transport ride that on his arrival he looked like a wild man, but after the company barber cut it he somehow looked even worse. It was impossible to find an army-issue shirt to fit him, because his neck was out of proportion to his arms and his arms were out of proportion to his torso. The company tailor reworked some shirts for him that at last fitted him after a fashion; even so, according to Lord, the shirts—on Prince—looked like pup tents.

The rest of us in the company talked a lot about our homes, our families, our school life back in civilian days, and other familiar things. One of the recurring topics among us was why we had joined the army in the first place. We were all very frank about it. Sometimes it had been family trouble, sometimes girl trouble, sometimes school trouble; but mostly, instead of being trouble, it had been the noonday demons of pure restlessness that drive young men to do despairing things. But Prince, though we gave him plenty of opportunity, would never say why he had enlisted for the 15th Infantry, that fabulous outfit—according to the recruiting sergeants back in the States—which was a sort of American Foreign Legion quartered in a land of tiled walls and jeweled pagodas where almond-eyed men with pigtails wore womanish gowns, drank tea, ate rice, smoked opium, and wielded beheading knives. In fact, Prince rarely said anything at all, and always seemed wrapped in a shroud of moroseness. In his free time, he would either lie on his bunk or sit gloomily and silently in the dayroom. He never received any letters, and he never wrote any. He never read a book or a magazine. He never played pool or checkers. He never accompanied us to the bars, or went with us on strolls through the beautiful parks of Tientsin. Martin Lord, logically embittered, said Prince had no sense of smell, no sense of taste, no sense of feeling, no sense.

Clumsy in everything, Prince was clumsiest of all with the Springfield rifle, in those days the queen of the foot soldier's arms. Usually, after practicing enough and absorbing enough bawlings out from his instructors, a recruit could learn to do a fair job of inspection arms, right or left shoulder arms, present arms, order arms, and the other things one does in rifle drill. But not Prince. The intricacies of flipping his Springfield about in unison with his mates were forever beyond his ability to grasp. After about two months, it became so evident that Prince would never make a soldier that Captain Hauser relieved him of regular duty and assigned him permanently to the supply room, overriding the outraged protests of the supply sergeant. In the supply room, Prince did such things as sort tent pegs and canteens. Mostly, he just sat around. He didn't mind. He hated drill, anyway.

In July, we left for summer camp for shooting on the target range. If you made Expert Rifleman, your pay went up five dollars a month. If you made Sharpshooter, your pay went up three dollars. If you made Marksman, your pay didn't go up but you did get a medal, for you had qualified with the Springfield. It was the aim of every company commander to see that his outfit qualified a hundred per cent. Of course, the more Experts and Sharpshooters he ended up with, the better, but his paramount desire was to boast of a company with no bolos in it—men who couldn't hit the target.

We went through endless sighting-in sessions and trigger-squeezing exercises before we ever fired a live cartridge. The bodily positions we practiced taking were as formalized as those taught to a ballet dancer. The feet had to be placed at a certain angle, the wrists had to be cocked a certain way, the elbows had to assume just the right crook. Furthermore, the rifle's sling had to be adjusted with the tightest nicety around one's arm, and the rifle's sights set with the precision of a micrometer. One had to practice holding one's breath before squeezing the trigger. Even one's psychological attitude had to be prepared. "You must learn to love up to that gun like you would to a sweet young girl," we were told.

We paired off in twos, one man coaching the other and then being coached in turn. We would encourage each other, correct each other, bawl each other out, and sometimes have fights. The dominating idea was to get in the best shape possible to hit the bull's-eye, and we put our hearts into the task. Martin Lord was paired off with Prince. Everybody in the regiment except the field grade officers had to fire for record, and Captain Hauser decided, if it was humanly possible for anyone to teach Prince how to shoot, Lord was the man to do it. Lord was the best shot in the company. Captain Hauser told Lord that if he could coach Prince into qualifying with the Springfield, he, Hauser, would promote Lord to corporal on the spot. Lord answered with a dubious "Yessir," and went at it.

At the end of the dry-run training period, Captain Hauser asked Lord what he thought Prince's chances were of qualifying.

"I don't know, sir," said Lord. "He's not coming along so good. He just lies there like a hog or something. He doesn't see any use for the rifle sling, and he claims he's got to shut one eye to see the target. He says the elbow pads in his shooting coat make his arms stiff. He can't see why he

shouldn't take the sitting position the way *he* wants to instead
of the way the book says. And I never have been able to
get it into his head that he's got to estimate the wind and
set his sights accordingly."

"Well, we start shooting live ammunition tomorrow," said
Captain Hauser. "He's got to fire along with everybody else.
Let's hope a miracle happens."

The first ten targets in the pits were assigned to our company. Accordingly, ten of our men, first group, took their
positions on the firing line and slipped clips of live ammunition
into their Springfields. The rifles had previously been "zeroed
in" by firing them from sandbag rests. Not even the worst
duffer could miss when he fired over a sandbag. Lord had
Target No. 1, Prince had Target No. 2. They were to begin
on the two-hundred-yard line and were to shoot standing. Each
man had his own little scorebook, and every shot he fired
was supposed to go down in that book. On each page was
a miniature target, and he was to note on that target where
every shot he fired hit. Thus he would keep a permanent
record of how he was grouping his shots and how much
windage and elevation it took to get a shot into the bull's-eye.

At a table behind each pair of men on the firing line, a third
man sat and kept their official scores—at this stage, their
practice scores. I sat behind Lord and Prince. Lord's first
shot was a twelve-o'clock four, which meant that the bullet
struck in the white just above the bull's-eye. Prince's first
shot struck the parapet in front of the pits and raised a
cloud of dust. Nobody said anything, because this was exactly
what had been expected. I marked Lord down for a four
and Prince for a zero. On his second shot, Lord got another
twelve-o'clock four.

"Lower your sights a degree, Lord," said Captain Hauser.
"Start getting them in there."

Prince fired again. This time no dust flew up, so we knew

he must have hit the target somewhere or gone completely over it.

"Call that shot, Prince," said Captain Hauser. In calling a shot, the rifleman sings out where he thinks the bullet has hit, basing his call on the alignment of his sights at the moment the rifle discharges.

"Right where I p'inted it," said Prince.

"That's no way to call a shot," said Captain Hauser. "Call it again. Call it properly, like you've been taught."

"Right where I p'inted it, at the black spot," said Prince stubbornly.

Captain Hauser started to let loose a verbal blast, but then Prince's target slid up. It was marked with a white spotter, and the spotter was in the center of the bull's-eye. Captain Hauser blew out his breath. "Keep pointing them that way, and everything will be all right," he said.

Prince did so. When he had finished his string of ten shots, he had scored nine bull's-eyes, which, with his first deplorable miss, gave him a total of forty-five. Lord had a total of forty-two.

We told each other as we moved back to the three-hundred-yard line that Prince was one of those freaks with a natural aptitude for shooting offhand at two hundred yards but that after we got back to the five- and six-hundred-yard lines, where you really had to "hold 'em and squeeze 'em," he wouldn't do so well. But he did. He made so many bull's-eyes that it became monotonous to watch him. When the firing was over for the day, his practice score was the highest not only for our company but for the whole battalion.

Lord, hopeful once again of getting his corporal's stripes, was nevertheless as puzzled by Prince's showing as was everyone else. "I sure can't figure it out," he said. "He doesn't adjust his sights or anything. He just holds a little higher or a little lower or a little to the left or to the right. That's what they call taking Kentucky windage, like they did back in the days of the old flintlock squirrel rifles. He never used his scorebook once all day, either. He claims it doesn't mean anything to mark your shots down."

Kentucky windage or no, Prince had demonstrated that he was a brilliant rifle shot, and everybody admitted it. We sought, in a fumbling way, to congratulate him. He looked at us with his usual dull, stupid stare and said, "I just p'int 'em where I want 'em to go. I never knowed that first time that I was supposed to hit that black spot."

"Yes, but you must have shot a lot before this, didn't you?" I said.

"Naw," he said. "My maw wouldn't never allow firearms around."

When we shot a few days later for the official record, Prince, of course, qualified as an Expert Rifleman. His score was 330 out of a possible 350 and was the best made that summer in the entire 15th Infantry. He was named along with Lord and a dozen other Experts in the regiment to make up the rifle team that would later compete, on this same firing range, with the marines from the United States Legation guard in Peking for the service championship of North China. Everyone was certain that with Prince on the team the 15th would swamp the marines this time, although we had been beaten in most of the previous years.

Our company returned to Tientsin, leaving Prince and Lord behind to practice with the regimental team. Three weeks later, the day the big match was to be fired, some Medical Corps men brought Prince back to Tientsin and carried him to the Compound hospital for an emergency operation. He had refused to leave his bunk that morning, saying, when questioned by the rifle-team captain, "Something's hurting in my guts." It had been an eight-hour train ride from Chingwangtao to Tientsin, and he died that night on the operating table. His appendix had ruptured.

Next day, Lord came back from Chingwangtao, where

the 15th Infantry rifle team had, as usual, lost to the marines. Captain Hauser accosted Lord about Prince. "The surgeon says he must have been in pain for days. Didn't he ever complain about it?"

"He never said a single damn word, sir," said Lord. "He never said anything until the morning of the match, when he couldn't leave his bunk. That guy never had any nerves. That's why he was such a good shot. He couldn't even feel the kick of a Springfield, and when you can't feel that you can't feel anything."

At Prince's funeral service, on the parade ground of the Compound, the chaplain preached, eight of us formed a firing squad and gave him three final volleys, and Taps was blown. Then his coffin was stowed away at an undertaking establishment until transportation could be arranged to take his body back to the States.

Captain Hauser sent off a cablegram to Prince's mother, having found her name and address in Prince's enlistment papers. Then he decided to make up a package of mementos concerning Prince and send that to his mother also. He told those of us who had been Prince's squadmates to contribute whatever we could find to go into the package. None of us contributed anything, because none of us had anything— not a single picture of him (and we were always getting our pictures taken), not a single souvenir, not anything at all. Captain Hauser searched Prince's foot locker and wall locker. There was nothing in them except his army-issue clothing, and very little of that. Not a single letter. Not a single photograph. Everyone else had Chinese knickknacks he had picked up here and there; everyone else had a scrapbook of sorts that he kept. But not Prince. He had nothing.

Captain Hauser then thought of the Expert Rifleman's medal that Prince had won on the range at Chingwangtao but which, because of his death, had never been presented to him. Captain Hauser got one from the supply sergeant and wrote out an elaborate presentation order to go with it.

"Now then," he said to those of us in Prince's squad, "I want each of you men to sit down and write a little note to this boy's mother. You can say you were pals with him and liked him and enjoyed his company, and all that sort of thing. You can tell some little anecdotes about him that will please her. Get at it right away, because I want to get the package with his medal in it off today, and I want to put your letters in it."

We tried. At first we were stumped. There was just nothing to write—no anecdote to put down about a fellow that we hadn't liked in the first place and who had lain gloomily on his bunk while the rest of us were out enjoying ourselves. Then, the way most people do in such circumstances, we made up things about Prince, but after we put them down on paper we saw how false they looked and we couldn't bring ourselves to let them be sent.

Finally, Martin Lord had an idea. "It's a round robin," he said. "I saw one somewhere before." He took a sheet of paper and in the center of it printed:

He was the best
rifle shot we
fellows ever saw.

"Now," he said, "we'll all sign our names in a circle around it, and the captain can send it off. It's a round robin."

We did so reluctantly, for, being army men, we hated to sign our names to anything, even to such an innocent thing as this. We took the paper to Captain Hauser and told him it was the best we could do.

He looked at it, looked at us, and said, "I can't send that boy's mother any such fool thing as this." Then his face screwed up in that peculiar way children's do when they are about to cry. He seemed to realize that this was all we could come up with, and at the same time he seemed moved by the awful blankness of it, by the thought of the dead boy who was getting no better tribute than this. Then he said, "Yes, I can send it, too. I'll wrap his Expert's medal in it."

He wrapped it, but he never sent it. A cablegram came later that day in reply to the one he had sent to Prince's mother to notify her of her son's death. It was from the Red Cross in Prince's home town. It said that Prince's mother had died a month before he enlisted and that there were no surviving relatives. Somehow—for some reason—he had given her name in his enlistment papers even though she was dead. Prince's body was finally buried in the army cemetery at the presidio in San Francisco, a scant few miles from the pier where, a few months before, he had embarked for China.

THE OLD FOGIES

2 ❅

The 15th always celebrated May 4 in proper style. May 4 was Organization Day, the day when, back in 1861, Abraham Lincoln had constituted the regiment a regular unit in the United States Army. The Day in Tientsin started off with a regimental parade and review in the Compound in front of stands set up for the officers' families and civilian spectators. Review and parade over, we formed a hollow square, stood at ease, and listened as, by custom, the regimental commander gave the *Address*. On one Organization Day General Castner decided to give the *Address* himself instead of leaving it up to the colonel. He did so, devoting some thirty minutes to the evils of venereal disease, a subject his listeners in the stands—mostly women—thought singularly inappropriate. When the colonel gave the *Address*, however, it was usually just a sort of pep talk designed to spur us on to greater effort.

After the *Address* had been delivered, the senior staff officer would read the *History of the Regiment*, a document which had begun to be compiled at Shiloh and which dwindled out at Tientsin, but which, the staff officer pointed out, was of necessity incomplete, for greater glories and greater things awaited the regiment in the future when the next big war should break out. He was right. In 1942, for instance, as part of the Third Division, the regiment would land in North Africa, and in the fighting which followed in Italy, France, and Germany, sixteen members of it would win the Congressional Medal of Honor.

The talks over and forgotten, the regiment staged an athletic field day with much business of hundred-yard dashing, pole vaulting, high jumping, relaying, and hurdling. That done with, the troops sat down—by that time rather winded and listless—to their holiday dinner. In the afternoon, flowers were sent to the wife of the regimental commander in the name of the officers of the regiment. In the evening, a dinner and dance were held for the officers and ladies of the regiment. For the enlisted men and their friends and wives—if any—tepid entertainment was offered at the YMCA across the street from the Compound. Relatively few of us ever took advantage of it, preferring to make a round of the bars instead.

On the first Organization Day I underwent after joining the regiment, I did my proper share of parading and passing in review and listening to the *Address* and the *History of the Regiment*, but, because I could neither hurdle, high jump, pole vault, nor dash a hundred yards with any distinction, I was only a spectator—along with about seven hundred and fifty others—at the athletic events. In the stands, during the parade and review, I had noticed a small group of men sitting off by themselves. They wore army uniforms of a most out-of-date mode, some of them, indeed, being dressed in the old infantry blues which had been discarded long before the First World War. I asked Corporal Brutschi who they were.

"Them guys?" he said contemptuously. "They're just the Old Fogies. They show up every time we put on a parade. They got nothing else to do."

"Yes, but who are they? How'd they get here?"

"They got here like anybody else. They come on boats. Don't be so dumb."

I took my inquiries elsewhere and finally found out that the Old Fogies (actually, the liberal infantrymen gave them a grosser name) were retired army men who had chosen to live out their lives among the fleshpots of North China rather than back in the States. They had an exclusive club of their own where they played checkers and poker, shot pool, read newspapers, and took their meals and did their drinking. Some of them lived alone, others with squaws. These squaws, according to the taste of the Old Fogy, might be Chinese or Japanese or Korean or German or White Russian or, in at least one case, French. The majority were Chinese, some of them startlingly young. The Old Fogies' retirement pay, which would have been only a pittance in the States, was magnified at least three and a half times by exchanging it into Chinese money, and the Old Fogies and their squaws lived very well indeed. If the Fogies got sick, the Post Hospital was open to them. They could buy their razor blades and soap and cigarettes at cost in the Post Exchange.

The club, as such, had been formed around 1915 by some old-timers who had retired from the 15th, but who had stayed on in Tientsin instead of returning to the States. All these founding Fogies had squaws, which was one of the reasons why they had remained in Tientsin, and they decided to set up a meeting place where the squaws would not be allowed to enter and where a man could act like an American once in a while. Individually, they didn't have much buying power, but, by pooling their resources, they managed to open their club. Over the years, by simple accretion, it had developed into the haven which it was in 1927.

The Fogies had it made, as the saying goes, and they knew it. But, also, they were a closed corporation. General Castner, after he took over command of the United States Army Forces in North China, sized them up one day, discovered how their ranks were recruited, and decided to put a stop to it.

The recruiting worked this way: An Old Fogy would know a sergeant, say, back in the States who had twenty-seven or more army years to his credit and was loafing out the last two or three until the thirty-year mark should be reached and he could retire. The Old Fogy would write him a letter about the delights of retired life in Tientsin, and the aging sergeant in the States, if the idea enticed him, thereupon would put in for transfer in grade to the 15th Infantry. Usually there would be several sergeants in the regiment who hated both the 15th and China, and the transfer would be arranged to the mutual satisfaction of both parties. The young, unhappy sergeant would go back to the States, and the old codger would replace him in the 15th. There he would dodder out his remaining two or three army years, coax a first sergeant or a master sergeant to step down for him on his last day in the service, and retire at top or near-top retirement pay with the whole regiment marching in review for him, and the colonel shaking his hand and giving a short talk on how the army was the poorer for losing such a man. Then the retiree would pack his kit, leave the regimen of Reveille and Taps forever, and move into his previously selected shack with his previously selected squaw, and become a member of the Old Fogies' Club.

General Castner's attitude was that this system, commendable as it might seem to potential Fogies, was loading the non-commissioned echelons of the United States Army Forces in China with the decrepit and the infirm and the muddle-headed, whereas what he wanted was youth and vigor and intelligence. So he issued an order that no more replacements over thirty-five years of age would be accepted for China duty, and that men who had served in China for nine years had to go home. As for the Old Fogies themselves, he couldn't touch them, and they knew it; and although they still had to salute him, they always managed when they did so to convey the impression that, at the same time, they were calling him a dirty name. Castner, as old as many of the Fogies themselves, recognized this and retaliated by summoning them to the side of his Cadillac whenever he passed them on the streets and bawling them out about their appearance or general behavior. Then Castner would go his way and the Fogies would go theirs, with no thought of appeasement on either side.

The Fogies made a practice of repelling advances from the members of the 15th; they didn't want young soldiers cluttering up the bar of their club; they didn't want any lecherous eyes made at their squaws. I gained entry only once to their mysterious clubrooms and that was through the magic key of literature.

The Tientsin Bookstore, in those days, was one of the great bookstores of the world; you could get anything there, in any language. It was there that I purchased my first copy of Joyce's *Ulysses*, the famed "4th Printing" by Shakespeare and Company of Paris, dated January 1924. The book by then, after suffering burnings in New York and seizures in Folkstone, was universally banned throughout the English-speaking world. But in Tientsin nothing was banned. A small, stout, past middle-age man, neatly dressed in a blue serge suit, was in the store when I made the purchase. He wanted some book which he couldn't properly identify. The multilingual Chinese clerk didn't seem to know what he was talking about.

"There's a lord and lady in it; that's about all I know," said the blue-serged man. Inspiredly, I said to the clerk, "I think he means *Lady Chatterley's Lover*." The clerk shrugged and offered him a copy. It was the Italian edition, printed in English, of course, but abounding in typographical errors, and it was the first version. Lawrence was to rewrite it twice before he was satisfied with it. It wasn't the book the blue-serged man had been looking for, but, after he scanned some of the pages toward the rear, he decided to buy it anyway; and, with our books under our arms, we left the Tientsin Bookstore together.

"This'll give me something to read tonight when I'm having my steak," he said. "Thanks for lending me a hand."

"Are you in business here?" I asked.

"Hell no, I'm not in business. I'm Master Sergeant George Smith, retired. I'm what you young devils call an Old Fogy."

I couldn't think of anything to say to that but "Oh, yes. Of course." Except for exchanging a few civilities when we parted, our friendship didn't exactly flourish that day; but later on, months later, once again I met Master Sergeant George Smith in the Tientsin Bookstore. I had just bought Huysmans' *Against the Grain*. Smith came up to me, just as if we had been pals for years, and said, "That Chatterley book was all right now; I liked the way it was written. I don't think it would be good for kids, but for an old fella that's been around . . . why, it's interesting. I read it three times. I never had much time for reading when I was in the army, but I got plenty of time now. The books in the YMCA library are just a little bit sissified. Do you suppose they got any more books here sort of like that Chatterley one?"

"Stacks of them," I said. And I spoke with authority, for I had looked them over many times. I led him to a table where there was a copy of Frank Harris' *Life and Loves*.

He thumbed through it a bit—he had the knack of being able to read rapidly—and he shut it with a snap and said, "I'll take it." And he didn't even flinch when the Chinese clerk told him the price.

The third time I met him—a week later—was outside the Old Fogies' Club itself. "Well!" he said. "Well! I've been looking for you. I wanted to discuss that book of Harris'. Why, it's just brilliant in spots. Brilliant. Come in, get out of the dust and the stink, and have a beer."

"I thought us fellows weren't very welcome in your club," I said, indicating my uniform.

"Lad," he replied, "you're welcome anywhere in this whole damn town when you're with Master Sergeant George Smith. Come on in and get out of the dust."

So we entered the Old Fogies' Club. The Chinese No. 1 boy popped up immediately with a big, raggedy ledger in his hand—the Old Fogies' guest book. Master Sergeant Smith signed for me and for himself in neat, crabbed handwriting. "Now, get us some beer and be quick about it," he snapped at the No. 1 boy.

The dayroom of the club, as the Fogies called it, was beautiful. There were rugs on the floors, and the walls were of yellow bamboo inlay set between black beams. The chairs were deep, reclining ones, upholstered in gold-colored leather. In niches in the walls were little Chinese statues. A rack of newspapers stood behind a Chinese screen. By each chair was a lacquered taboret with an ashtray on it. There was a life-sized photograph on the far wall. It was a picture of a nude girl, standing, her hair flowing down over her shoulders and arms to her hips. It was impossible to tell what nationality she was.

Three or four of the Fogies were in their favorite chairs with their favorite drinks beside them on the taborets. They looked at me unfriendly and at Smith critically. It all reminded me—except for the life-sized photo—of a cartoon

I had seen in *Punch* of a British officers' club, where the old colonels and generals sat grumpily with their whiskies and sodas and frowned in silence at an intruder.

Smith introduced me all around: "Master Sergeant this . . . Technical Sergeant that . . . First Sergeant this . . ." They were all dressed in civilian clothes and wore their coats and neckties. Each one stood up and shook hands perfunctorily and sat down again promptly. They hated, and took no pains to conceal it, any upsetting of their stated hours. Some of them were much older than I had supposed them to be when I had seen them from a distance as they sat in their isolated group in the reviewing stand when we were having a parade. In fact, one of the first sergeants reminded me immediately of Jonathan Swift's immortal Struldbrugs, even to having the distinguishing coal-black mark on his forehead as large as an English shilling.

The bamboo, the black beams, and the wood in the dayroom had that soft, deep patina which wood only achieves after it has been gone over every day, year after long year, with a soft waxy cloth. It looks eternal.

The club, Master Sergeant Smith explained to me, was run on strict military lines. You could not expect old soldiers to do otherwise. A sergeant major was in general charge of the club's management, and did the hiring and firing of the Chinese servant personnel. A finance sergeant kept the club's books. The members signed chits for their meals and drinks and paid up once a month to him. Some of them even authorized him to draw their retirement pay for them, deduct their debts from it at the end of the month, and bank the remainder for them. A mess sergeant bought their food and oversaw the cooking of it. A pill roller (retired Medical Corps man) looked after their minor ills. The only thing they didn't have was a chaplain. But some of them were religious men and read their Bibles.

The main clubroom, as I have said, was the dayroom.

The dining room was the mess hall. The toilet was the head. The sleeping quarters on the second floor for those who chose to live at the club rather than to shack up was the barracks, a series of screened-off rooms each with its window, its neat army bunk, its foot and wall lockers, its washbowl and slop jar.

They had a tailor who made civilian clothes for them and kept their beloved old uniforms in repair. They had a barber who shaved them every day and gave them haircuts when needed. When one of them died—which was a very rare thing—he was given a military funeral in the 15th's Compound, complete with rifle salute and Taps and the chaplain's prayers, and, unless he had relatives in the States to claim his body, was buried in the Race Course Road Cemetery, where lay so many American casualties of the Boxer Uprising.

Retired pay for the Fogies averaged about four hundred Chinese dollars a month. Some of the more frugal ones, when they died, left distant inlaws in the States as much as a thousand dollars American.

If they shacked up, their squaws were usually given a hundred dollars Chinese a month to run the shacks, neat two- or three-room apartments in compounds down the street from the club. This monthly hundred dollars represented wealth, when one considers that the average coolie in Tientsin in those days grossed less than eighteen dollars American a year. Some of the Fogies liked their squaws so much that they settled down to be "old married men" with market baskets. Some of them even went through marriage ceremonies. Some of them sired children.

The original squaws back in the days when the club first had been formed had been recruited from the brothels. As the years went on, squawdom became almost economic queendom, and the taking of a squaw was merely a matter of exercising one's choice among a multitude of candidates frankly offered by the relatives of the current kept women.

All the Fogies were confirmed and well-practiced remi-
niscers. In their dayroom, waited on watchfully by their
servants, they talked endlessly and with savage enthusiasm
of the outfits they had served in and the battles they had
fought. They were very scornful of us young men of the
15th Infantry, for our military memories were only of
two or three or five years in uniform, whereas theirs were
of lifetimes.

They loved food, and their mess was the peer of any
hotel's in Tientsin. Their ancient tummies relished soups,
the subtle soups that only the great cookery of North China
could create. They liked rice, too; it was easy for their
sometimes toothless gums to masticate. But they also loved
fish, and the beef from Australia, and pork and chicken and
duck and frog legs from Hopei Province, and lamb from
New Zealand, and bacon from Scandinavia. Their butter,
coffee, and sugar they bought in the 15th's Commissary.
Their mess sergeant always made their bread himself, a
crusty bread, good to dip in soup, which he had learned to
make when he was a young man in Paris.

They paid no taxes. They respected no authority except
their own, but a lifetime in the army had taught them that
authority was as necessary as personal cleanliness. So they
maintained a vague military tribunal among themselves. No
one outside the ranks of the Fogies ever found out exactly
how it operated, but if one of their members fell out of line
and sinned against their code, attention was brought in some
manner to the U. S. Consulate, and the old delinquent was
sent home.

Several times Master Sergeant Smith invited me to his
shack to drink wine and discuss books. The shack was a
three-room apartment on the fourth floor of a brick building known colloquially as the House of All Nations because
of the racially mixed families that lived there. The rooms,

one occupied by Smith, one by his squaw, and the third serving as kitchen, dining room and room-of-all-trades, opened on a veranda where one could stand and look out on the city. Most visible of all was the American flag, flying from its staff on top of the water tower in the 15th Infantry Compound.

His squaw was a Manchurian girl, rather tall. On my first visit she was dressed in a flowered gown and, on a small stove over a coal fire, was preparing fried pork and noodles. She never spoke a word then or during any of my other visits, but as soon as we came in she brought us wrung-out hot towels with which to bathe our faces. When Smith sat down and opened a bottle of sauterne, she stood behind him and massaged his neck and shoulder blades; and, when she had finished with his, came over and stood behind me and massaged mine.

"She paints, too," said Smith at the time of my first visit, and, from a cabinet, he took out a scroll about ten inches high and ten feet long. In classic Chinese manner, the painting began at the right, and the story it told unfolded as the scroll was unrolled. The opening scene was of the mouth of a river: cannon mounted in forts there were firing at warships out to sea. "Taku," said Smith. "You know—at the mouth of the Hai Ho where those busted-up guns emplacements are. This shows the opening shots of the Boxer business." As he unrolled the scroll, the foreign armies fought their way up the Hai River and battled it out with the Boxers in Tientsin and raised the siege of Peking. "I told her about it, and she painted it," said Smith. "She wasn't even born then. You see, I fought in that particular scrap myself. That's supposed to be me there—the guy with the flag."

After I returned to the States and was mustered out of the army, Smith and I corresponded intermittently over the years. The last letter I received from him was in 1937. He said there were rumors that the 15th would be pulled out of China soon "to avoid an incident," that the Japs were acting cockier every day, and that American civilians were being advised to leave China. He said some of the Fogies were making plans to get out, but the majority, including himself, thought they would stick it out. At the worst, all the Japs could do would be to intern them. Anyhow, who was afraid of a damned Jap?

In 1938, the 15th U. S. Infantry Regiment ended its twenty-six-year stay in North China and returned to the United States. Later that year, Tientsin fell to the armed forces of Japan.

Smith's dates: Born 1872. Enlisted in the army 1893. Fought in the Boxer Rebellion 1900 (when he first saw Tientsin). Fought in Mexico in the punitive expedition against Villa 1916. Trained World War I recruits at Jefferson Barracks 1917–18. Returned to the 15th and Tientsin in the grade of duty sergeant 1920. Retired from the army in Tientsin in the grade of master sergeant 1923. Died (?)